MACMILLAN MASTER GUIDES

ROMEO AND JULIET

BY WILLIAM SHAKESPEARE

HELEN MORRIS

D0348284

MACMILLAN

© Helen Morris 1985

All rights reserved. No reproduction, copy or transmission of this publication may be made without written permission.

No paragraph of this publication may be reproduced, copied or transmitted save with written permission or in accordance with the provisions of the Copyright, Designs and Patents Act 1988, or under the terms of any licence permitting limited copying issued by the Copyright Licensing Agency, 90 Tottenham Court Road, London W1P 9HE.

Any person who does any unauthorised act in relation to this publication may be liable to criminal prosecution and civil claims for damages.

First published 1985 by
MACMILLAN PRESS LTD
Houndmills, Basingstoke, Hampshire RG21 6XS
and London
Companies and representatives
throughout the world

ISBN 0–333–37288–3

A catalogue record for this book is available
from the British Library.

14 13 12 11 10 9 8 7 6 5
05 04 03 02 01 00 99 98 97 96

Printed in Malaysia

CONTENTS

General editor's preface   v

An introduction to the study of Shakespeare's plays   vi

1   **William Shakespeare:**
    life and career   1

2   **Elizabethan theatre**   2.1 Shakespeare's contacts   3
                                   2.2 'The Theatre'   3
                                   2.3 Shakespeare's company   4
                                   2.4 Shakespeare's texts   4

3   **Treatment of sources**   3.1 The plot   7
                                   3.2 Sources   7
                                   3.3 Speed of the action   8

4   **Themes**   4.1 Civil disorder   10
                                   4.2 Love and hate   11
                                   4.3 The 'generation gap'   12
                                   4.4 Fortune and fate   12
                                   4.5 Is the play a tragedy?   14

5   **Summary and commentary**   16

6   **Characterisation**   50

7   **The play on the stage**   7.1 Stage history   61
                                  7.2 Shakespeare's theatre   63
                                  7.3 Shakespeare's stagecraft   64
                                  7.4 Dramatic irony   64
                                  7.5 Establishing place   65
                                  7.6 Establishing time   67

8   **How the play is written**   8.1 Varieties of blank verse   69
                                  8.2 Word-play   70
                                  8.3 Images   71
                                  8.4 Lyric poetry   72
                                  8.5 Critical analysis of two passages 73

9   **Critical reception**   78

Revision questions   80
Appendix: Shakespeare's Theatre   81
Further reading   85

GENERAL EDITOR'S PREFACE

The aim of the Macmillan Master Guides is to help you to appreciate the book you are studying by providing information about it and by suggesting ways of reading and thinking about it which will lead to a fuller understanding. The section on the writer's life and background has been designed to illustrate those aspects of the writer's life which have influenced the work, and to place it in its personal and literary context. The summaries and critical commentary are of special importance in that each brief summary of the action is followed by an examination of the significant critical points. The space which might have been given to repetitive explanatory notes has been devoted to a detailed analysis of the kind of passage which might confront you in an examination. Literary criticism is concerned with both the broader aspects of the work being studied and with its detail. The ideas which meet us in reading a great work of literature, and their relevance to us today, are an essential part of our study, and our Guides look at the thought of their subject in some detail. But just as essential is the craft with which the writer has constructed his work of art, and this is considered under several technical headings – characterisation, language, style and stagecraft.

The authors of these Guides are all teachers and writers of wide experience, and they have chosen to write about books they admire and know well in the belief that they can communicate their admiration to you. But you yourself must read and know intimately the book you are studying. No one can do that for you. You should see this book as a lamppost. Use it to shed light, not to lean against. If you know your text and know what it is saying about life, and how it says it, then you will enjoy it, and there is no better way of passing an examination in literature.

JAMES GIBSON

Acknowledgement. Cover illustration: *Romeo and Juliet* by Ferdinand Piloty. courtesy of the Governors of the Royal Shakespeare Theatre. The drawing of the Globe Theatre is by courtesy of Alec Pearson.

AN INTRODUCTION TO THE STUDY OF SHAKESPEARE'S PLAYS

A play as a work of art exists to the full only when performed. It must hold the audience's attention throughout the performance, and, unlike a novel, it can't be put down and taken up again. It is important to experience the play as if you are seeing it on the stage for the first time, and you should begin by reading it straight through. Shakespeare builds a play in dramatic units which may be divided into smaller subdivisions, or episodes, marked off by exits and entrances and lasting as long as the same actors are on the stage. Study it unit by unit.

The first unit provides the exposition which is designed to put the audience into the picture. In the second unit we see the forward movement of the play as one situation changes into another. The last unit in a tragedy or a tragical play will bring the catastrophe and in comedy – and some of the history plays – an unravelling of the complications, what is called a *dénouement*.

The onward movement of the play from start to finish is its progressive structure. We see the chain of cause and effect (the plot) and the progressive revelation and development of character. The people, their characters and their motives drive the plot forward in a series of scenes which are carefully planned to give variety of pace and excitement. We notice fast-moving and slower-moving episodes, tension mounting and slackening, and alternate fear and hope for the characters we favour. Full-stage scenes, such as stately councils and processions or turbulent mobs, contrast with scenes of small groups or even single speakers. Each of the scenes presents a deed or event which changes the situation. In performance, entrances and exits and stage actions are physical facts, with more impact than on the page. That impact Shakespeare relied upon, and we must restore it by an effort of the imagination.

Shakespeare's language is just as diverse. Quickfire dialogue is followed by long speeches, and verse changes to prose. There is a wide range of speech – formal, colloquial, dialect, 'Mummerset' and the broken English of foreigners, for example. Songs, instrumental music, and the noise of battle, revelry and tempest, all extend the range of dramatic expression. The dramatic use of language is enhanced by skilful stagecraft, by costumes, by properties such as beds, swords and Yorick's skull, by such stage business as kneeling, embracing and giving money, and by use of such features of the stage structure as the balcony and the trapdoor.

By these means Shakespeare's people are brought vividly to life and cleverly individualised. But though they have much to tell us about human nature, we must never forget that they are characters in a play, not in real life. And remember, they exist to enact the play, not the play to portray *them*.

Shakespeare groups his characters so that they form a pattern, and it is useful to draw a diagram showing this. Sometimes a linking character has dealings with each group. The pattern of persons belongs to the symmetric structure of the play, and its dramatic unity is reinforced and enriched by a pattern of resemblances and contrasts; for instance, between characters, scenes, recurrent kinds of imagery, and words. It is not enough just to notice a feature that belongs to the symmetric structure, you should ask what its relevance is to the play as a whole and to the play's ideas.

These ideas and the dramatising of them in a central theme, or several related to each other, are a principal source of the dramatic unity. In order to see what themes are present and important, look, as before, for pattern. Observe the place in it of the leading character. In tragedy this will be the protagonist, in comedy heroes and heroines, together with those in conflict or contrast with them. In *I Henry IV*, Prince Hal is being educated for kingship and has a correct estimate of honour, while Falstaff despises honour, and Hotspur makes an idol of it. Pick out the episodes of great intensity as, for example, in *King Lear* where the theme of spiritual blindness is objectified in the blinding of Gloucester, and, similarly, note the emphases given by dramatic poetry as in Prospero's 'Our revels now are ended. . .' or unforgettable utterances such as Lear's 'Is there any cause in Nature that makes these hard hearts?' Striking stage-pictures such as that of Hamlet behind the King at prayer will point to leading themes, as will all the parallels and recurrences, including those of phrase and imagery. See whether, in the play you are studying, themes known to be favourites with Shakespeare are prominent, themes such as those of order and disorder, relationships disrupted by mistakes about identity, and appearance and reality. The latter were bound to fascinate Shakespeare whose theatrical art worked by means of illusions which pointed beyond the surface of actual life to underlying truths. In looking at themes beware of attempts to make the play fit some orthodoxy a critic believes in – Freudian perhaps, or Marxist, or dogmatic Christian theology – and remember that its ideas, though they often have a bearing on ours, are Elizabethan.

Some of Shakespeare's greatness lies in the good parts he wrote for the actors. In his demands upon them, and the opportunities he provided, he bore their professional skills in mind and made use of their physical prowess, relished by a public accustomed to judge fencing and wrestling as expertly as we today judge football and tennis. As a member of the professional group of players called the Chamberlain's Men he knew each actor he was writing for. To play his women he had highly-trained boys. As paired heroines they were often contrasted, short with tall, for example, or one vivacious and enterprising, the other more conventionally feminine.

Richard Burbage, the company's leading man, was famous as a great tragic actor, and he took leading roles in seven of Shakespeare's *tragedies*. Though each of the seven has its own distinctiveness, we shall find at the centre of all of them a tragic protagonist possessing tragic greatness, not just one 'tragic flaw' but a tragic vulnerability. He will have a character which makes him unfit to cope with the tragic situations confronting him, so that his tragic errors bring down upon him tragic suffering and finally a tragic catastrophe. Normally, both the suffering and the catastrophe are far worse than he can be said to deserve, and others are engulfed in them who deserve such a fate less or not at all. Tragic terror is aroused in us because, though exceptional, he is sufficiently near to normal humankind for his fate to remind us of what can happen to human beings like ourselves, and because we see in it a combination of inexorable law and painful mystery. We recognise the principle of cause and effect where in a tragic world errors return upon those who make them, but we are also aware of the tragic disproportion between cause and effect. In a tragic world you may kick a stone and start an avalanche which will destroy you and others with you. Tragic pity is aroused in us by this disproportionate suffering, and also by all the kinds of suffering undergone by every character who has won our imaginative sympathy. Imaginative sympathy is wider than moral approval, and is felt even if suffering does seem a just and logical outcome. In addition to pity and terror we have a sense of tragic waste because catastrophe has affected so much that was great and fine. Yet we feel also a tragic exaltation. To our grief the men and women who represented those values have been destroyed, but the values themselves have been shown not to depend upon success, nor upon immunity from the worst of tragic suffering and disaster.

Comedies have been of two main kinds, or cross-bred from the two. In critical comedies the governing aim is to bring out the absurdity or irrationality of follies and abuses, and make us laugh at them. Shakespeare's comedies often do this, but most of them belong primarily to the other kind – romantic comedy. Part of the romantic appeal is to our liking for suspense; they are dramas of averted threat, beginning in trouble and ending in joy. They appeal to the romantic senses of adventure and of wonder, and to complain that they are improbable is silly because the improbability, the marvellousness, is part of the pleasure. They dramatise stories of romantic love, accompanied by love doctrine – ideas and ideals of love. But they are plays in two tones, they are comic as well as romantic. There is often something to laugh at even in the love stories of the nobility and gentry, and just as there is high comedy in such incidents as the cross-purposes of the young Athenians in the wood, and Rosalind as 'Ganymede' teasing Orlando, there is always broad comedy for characters of lower rank. Even where one of the sub-plots has no effect on the main plot, it may take up a topic from it and present it in a more comic way.

What is there in the play to make us laugh or smile? We can distinguish many kinds of comedy it may employ. *Language* can amuse by its wit, or by absurdity, as in Bottom's malapropisms. Feste's nonsense-phrases, so fatuously admired by Sir Andrew, are deliberate, while his catechising of Olivia is clown-routine. Ass-headed Bottom embraced by the Fairy Queen is a *comic spectacle* combining costume and stage-business. His wanting to play every part is *comedy of character*. Phebe disdaining Silvius and in love with 'Ganymede', or Malvolio treating Olivia as though she had written him a love-letter is *comedy of situation*; the situation is laughably different from what Phebe or Malvolio supposes. A comic let-down or anticlimax can be devastating, as we see when Aragon, sure that he deserves Portia, chooses the silver casket only to find the portrait not of her but of a 'blinking idiot'. By *slapstick, caricature* or sheer *ridiculousness of situation*, comedy can be exaggerated into farce, which Shakespeare knows how to use on occasion. At the opposite extreme, before he averts the threat, he can carry it to the brink of tragedy, but always under control.

Dramatic irony is the result of a character or the audience anticipating an outcome which, comically or tragically, turns out very differently. Sometimes *we* foresee that it will. The speaker never foresees how ironical, looking back, the words or expectations will appear. When she says, 'A little water clears us of this deed' Lady Macbeth has no prevision of her sleep-walking words, 'Will these hands ne'er be clean?' There is irony in the way in which in all Shakespeare's tragic plays except *Richard II* comedy is found in the very heart of the tragedy. The Porter scene in *Macbeth* comes straight after Duncan's murder. In *Hamlet* and *Antony and Cleopatra* comic episodes lead into the catastrophe: the rustic Countryman brings Cleopatra the means of death, and the satirised Osric departs with Hamlet's assent to the fatal fencing match. The Porter, the Countryman and Osric are not mere 'comic relief', they contrast with the tragedy in a way that adds something to it, and affects our response.

A sense of the comic and the tragic is common ground between Shakespeare and his audience. Understandings shared with the audience are necessary to all drama. They include conventions, i.e. assumptions, contrary to what factual realism would demand, which the audience silently agrees to accept. It is, after all, by a convention, what Coleridge called a 'willing suspension of disbelief', that an actor is accepted as Hamlet. We should let a play teach us the conventions it depends on. Shakespeare's conventions allow him to take a good many liberties, and he never troubles about inconsistencies that wouldn't trouble an audience. What matters to the dramatist is the effect he creates. So long as we are responding as he would wish, Shakespeare would not care whether we could say by what means he has made us do so. But to appreciate his skill, and get a fuller understanding of his play, we have to distinguish these means, and find terms to describe them.

If you approach the Shakespeare play you are studying bearing in mind what is said to you here, then you will respond to it more fully than before. Yet like all works of artistic genius, Shakespeare's can only be analysed so far. His drama and its poetry will always have about them something 'which into words no critic can digest'.

HAROLD BROOKS

1 WILLIAM SHAKESPEARE: LIFE AND CAREER

We do not know the exact date of William Shakespeare's birth; he was baptised on 26 April 1564, and his birthday is nowadays celebrated on 23 April. It is appropriate that a playwright who spent so much time celebrating England should have his birthday on the day of England's patron saint, St George.

William's father, John Shakespeare, was a glover and leather merchant, dealing in purses, belts, gloves, aprons and the like, in Stratford-on-Avon, a market town in the heart of the English countryside. His mother's family were minor landed gentry and well-to-do farmers.

John Shakespeare for a time played a prominent part in local government, and became one of the fourteen principal burgesses, with a right to have his children educated freely at the 'King's New School'. In 1565 he became an alderman, and in 1568 was elected 'Bailiff' or mayor. But after 1576 John Shakespeare neglected council meetings, did not pay his dues, and in 1586 was replaced on the council because of 'non-attendance'.

William almost certainly went to the 'New School', which had at that time university graduates as teachers, and acquired the usual 'grammar school' education – in Latin, not English, grammar. Perhaps we can guess how little Elizabethan schoolboys enjoyed their schooling if we notice that every allusion to schoolboys in Shakespeare's plays emphasises their reluctance, 'creeping like snail unwillingly to school' (As You Like It, II.vii.146) and going 'toward school with heavy looks' (Romeo and Juliet, II.ii.157).

In November 1582 William married Anne Hathaway, who was some seven or eight years older, by special licence after only one calling of banns, and in May 1583 their daughter was born. Twins followed in February 1585, and were named Hamnet and Judith.

Shortly afterwards William Shakespeare left Stratford, and though much has been surmised, nothing is actually known of what he did during the next seven years. By 1592, however, the three parts of what was probably his first play, *Henry VI*, had appeared on the stage, and drawn comments from rival writers. Thomas Nashe had praised a scene in Part I, and Robert Greene had mocked the new 'Shake-scene', misquoting Part III.

Plague closed the theatres in 1593/94, and during these years Shakespeare published the only works which he himself saw through the press – two long, non-dramatic poems, *Venus and Adonis* and *The Rape of Lucrece*. By the time that the theatres reopened in 1594 Shakespeare was established as a member of the Lord Chamberlain's Company of actors, not a mere 'hired man' but a 'housekeeper' or 'sharer', owning part of the company and sharing any profits.

Shakespeare remained with this company throughout his professional career, until he retired to Stratford about 1611, the longest union of a playwright with a company of actors until that of Gilbert and Sullivan 300 years later.

All the time Shakespeare was working in London he was investing in property in Stratford, and when he retired he went there to live in New Place, one of the finest houses in the town. Shakespeare was now a respected and influential citizen of his native town, consulted about local matters such as the enclosure of common lands, which was being resisted by the citizens. Occasionally he visited London on business, and he did write part of a final play, *Henry VIII*, for the celebrations at the wedding of the Princess Elizabeth in 1613. Three years later he died, and, as a prominent citizen of the town, was buried in the chancel of the parish church.

2 ELIZABETHAN THEATRE

2.1 SHAKESPEARE'S CONTACTS

Despite a boyhood so far from London, Shakespeare had many opportunities of seeing actors at work. In *A Midsummer Night's Dream* (II.i.148) there seems to be a reference to a spectacle when in 1576 the Earl of Leicester entertained Queen Elizabeth at Kenilworth Castle (twelve miles from Stratford) for nineteen days, and people came from all the country round. In 1579 the great cycle of mystery plays was acted at Coventry. Touring companies visiting a town had to give their first performance before the council, to be approved, and many companies visited Stratford while John Shakespeare was a burgess. In 1583-4 three troupes performed in the Guild Hall, and between December 1586 and December 1587 five companies played in Stratford.

In 1583 the Master of the Revels at court had formed the Queen's Company from leading actors, the star being the famous comedian Richard Tarlton. When they were touring in 1587 one of the actors was killed in a brawl with another, at Thame; so when they came to Stratford (where they were paid twenty shillings, more than any other company had got) they were one man short. Was this a possible opening for Shakespeare?

2.2 'THE THEATRE'

Until 1576 the actors were accustomed to play wherever there was an audience, often in inn-yards, in local Guild Halls, on village greens, in the circular arenas used for bull- and bear-baiting, in the halls of manor houses and colleges. In London they used inn-yards; but these could be obstructed by carriers' carts, and they had to share the takings with the landlord. Also, within the city of London the Protestant authorities disapproved of acting, and harassed the players.

So in 1576 James Burbage, leader of Leicester's Men and father of the greatest Elizabethan actor, Richard Burbage, built a playhouse well outside the city walls, at Shoreditch. He called it 'The Theatre' and after it all our 'theatres' are named. It was such a success that a second playhouse, the Curtain, was built nearby. The name is misleading because it has nothing to do with stage curtains, which did not exist in the Elizabethan theatre, but simply came from the street in which it was situated, Curtain Close. In the winter, when the audience would not undertake the muddy trudge out to Shoreditch, the players still acted in the Cross Keys Inn in Gracious [Gracechurch] Street.

In 1599, after a dispute with the ground landlord, Shakespeare's Company tore down the Theatre, and rebuilt it on the south bank of the Thames, well outside the jurisdiction of the city. This was the Globe, perhaps the most famous theatre in the world. We shall see later how brilliantly Shakespeare made use of every feature in this theatre. (See page 64.)

2.3 SHAKESPEARE'S COMPANY

Actors and playwrights were very low on the social scale; indeed a law passed in 1572 bracketed them with rogues and vagabonds, who could be arrested unless they were servants 'to any Baron of this realm or . . . any person of greater degree'. So each company of actors had to find a patron. The first Lord Hunsdon, cousin of Queen Elizabeth and Lord Chamberlain, was patron of the company to which Shakespeare belonged.

He died in 1596 and his son took over the company as Lord Hunsdon's Men. In 1597 the second Lord Hunsdon became Lord Chamberlain, and the company once again became the Lord Chamberlain's Men. Finally, when James I came to the throne in 1603, they must have been London's leading company, for they were chosen to be his private company, the King's Men.

We do not know how good an actor Shakespeare was, though gossip has assigned to him very minor parts – the Ghost in *Hamlet* and Adam in *As You Like It*. We do know that he acted in at least two of Ben Jonson's plays, and in the First Folio (the collected edition of his plays published in 1623) his name heads the list of the 'principall Actors in all these plays' – a list of the twenty-six actors who had been 'sharers' in the company during the preceding thirty years.

2.4 SHAKESPEARE'S TEXTS

Shakespeare was not only an actor and 'sharer' in the management of the company, he was also their 'attached dramatist' or 'poet in ordinary'.

Such a writer was contracted to produce usually two, but sometimes three, plays a year, exclusively for his company. For this he got a weekly sslary and a benefit performance. He could not publish his work unless the company agreed – which they would not normally do, since if one of their plays was published, another company might perform it. Texts exist of less than twenty per cent of the plays of this period of which we know the titles, simply because so few were published. The manuscripts wore out, or got mislaid, and were lost. The Admiral's Men acted 215 plays between June 1594 and March 1603: fifteen survive.

The company owned the manuscripts, which explains why there is no mention of manuscripts in Shakespeare's will – but in any case a wealthy leading citizen in puritan Stratford (where by 1616 acting of plays was forbidden) would not want to remind people that he had once been a 'common player'.

He did leave money to buy mourning rings for three members of his company, old friends, Richard Burbage, John Heminge and Henry Condell. Some seven years after Shakespeare's death Heminge and Condell decided to collect and publish his plays – a rare tribute. They explained affectionately that they did it 'without ambition either of selfe-profit or fame; onely to keepe the memory of so worthy a Friend and Fellow alive, as was our Shakespeare'. Their collection of plays was published in 1623, and is called the First Folio.

Less than half of Shakespeare's plays were published in his lifetime, and it is unlikely that he had anything to do with those that did appear. They are mainly imperfect, unauthorised versions, which appeared singly in quarto size books, and are known as the Quartos.

Romeo and Juliet was probably written about 1595. It first appeared in print in 1597, without Shakespeare's name, and claimed to have been 'often (with great applause) plaid publiquely' by Lord Hunsdon's Servants – a name only used by the company from July 1596 to April 1597. This version, known as Q1, has 700 lines less than the complete play, and has various cuts which shorten it – for instance, I.i.147–157 and the Prologue to Act II – without interfering with the plot. Perhaps it is a version made for touring, because it can be acted with fewer players than the next version, Q2, published in 1599, and claiming to be 'newly corrected, augmented and amended'. In Q2, 'Here come the Capulets' is in Q1, 'Here comes a Capulet' and 'a serving man with logs and coals' in Q1 (IV.iv.14) is replaced in Q2 by 'three or four with spits and logs and baskets'. The text of Q1 is imperfect. The scenes in which Paris and/or Romeo appear are nearly word-perfect; the other seven are not. It seems that the play was written down and sold to the printer by the actors who played these parts and knew them well, but did not have by heart the scenes in which they were off the stage.

The actor might forget some of the words, but remember the action on the stage, and describe it in stage directions. For instance, in Q1 Juliet says, 'Father, hear me speak', and a stage direction follows: 'She kneels down'. In Q2 Juliet completes the speech 'Good Father, I, beseech you on my knees: the speech enforces the action, as so often in Shakespeare, and no stage direction is required.

The play was immensely popular; a third quarto, Q3, appeared in 1609, and is the text used for the authoritative First Folio. For those who could not afford the collected plays, two more quartos appeared before the theatres were closed in 1642.

3 TREATMENT OF SOURCES

3.1 THE PLOT

Romeo and Juliet is set in Verona, in Northern Italy. Two leading families, the Montagues and the Capulets, have a long-standing quarrel between them, and (to the annoyance of the Prince and the other citizens) members of these households cannot meet without brawling and disturbing the peace.

Capulet intends to marry his only daughter Juliet to the Prince's kinsman, Paris. But she and Romeo, a young Montague, fall in love at first sight, and persuade Friar Lawrence to marry them immediately. As he returns from his wedding Romeo is challenged by the quarrelsome Tybalt, a Capulet, but refuses to fight his new kinsman. Romeo's friend Mercutio fights instead, and is slain. Romeo avenges Mercutio by killing Tybalt, and is banished by the Prince.

Capulet proceeds with his plan to marry Juliet to Paris. Friar Lawrence tries to prevent this by supplying Juliet with a drug which will make her appear dead for forty-two hours; meanwhile he will send for Romeo to rescue her. The messenger is delayed; Romeo learns only that Juliet is dead, and determines to die with her. The mourning Paris tries to prevent Romeo breaking into Juliet's tomb, and is slain. Romeo poisons himself, and the waking Juliet, finding him dead, stabs herself with his dagger.

The Montague and Capulet parents are reconciled, but to no purpose, for all the younger generation are dead.

3.2 SOURCES

When he came to write *Romeo and Juliet* Shakespeare had already tried his hand at tragedy, in *Titus Andronicus* and *Richard III*. But these had plots of the usual pattern for tragedy, which recounted the fall of some great historical or classical figure, and the consequent distress caused to the society in which he lived. Love was considered a subject for comedy – lovers had comparatively slight troubles which could be cured, and the comedy could have a happy ending. Now Shakespeare wrote a new kind of tragedy. It was not about one 'hero' but about two young lovers, the heroine quite as important as the hero; their troubles led to their deaths, and this did not disrupt, but healed, a disordered society. It was fashionable to write 'revenge' plays, but as the critic Professor Levin has pointed out, *Romeo and Juliet* is an 'anti-revenge' play.

Shakespeare did not invent the plots of his plays. He found a likely theme in a chronicle, a poem or a book of tales or biographies, and re-created it to suit his own purposes. There are several earlier versions of the story of *Romeo and Juliet* in French and Italian; and it occurs in an English collection of prose stories which William Painter translated from the Italian in 1567, which Shakespeare may have read. But quite certainly he knew well the long poem – over 3 000 lines – written in 1562 by Arthur Brooke, and reissued in 1587: *The tragicall Historye of Romeus and Juliet*. Not only are many details of the plot the same, but Shakespeare's language and images often echo Brooke's. Another source is possible; Brooke tells us that he had already, in 1562, seen 'the same argument lately set forth on stage', and it is possible that Shakespeare had seen or heard of the same play, and borrowed from it parts of his *Romeo and Juliet* (for instance, the balcony scene) which do not occur in Brooke's poem. By noticing how Brooke's version is altered, and to what effect, we can perhaps discover what aspects of the story Shakespeare wished to emphasise.

3.3 SPEED OF THE ACTION

In Brooke's version the story moves at a leisurely pace over some nine months. The lovers meet at a masked ball, and fall in love, but 'a week or two' passes before Romeus dares to approach Juliet, whereas Shakespeare's Romeo does not wait more than an hour or two before climbing into the orchard. More weeks pass before Romeus' marriage, and months before he kills Tybalt, whereas Romeo kills Tybalt as he walks back from his wedding, the afternoon after he first met Juliet, and before his marriage is consummated.

Romeo and Juliet are well described by Rosalind, the heroine of *As You Like It*: they 'no sooner met, but they looked; no sooner looked, but they loved; no sooner loved, but they sighed; no sooner sighed but they asked one another the reason; no sooner knew the reason but they sought the remedy. . . they will together; clubs cannot part them' (V.ii.37).

The whole action of *Romeo and Juliet* takes place in five days, Sunday to Thursday.

It is not only the young lovers who are in a hurry. Juliet's father's haste to have her married to Paris speeds up the action:

CAPULET: . . .bid her, mark you me, on Wednesday next –
But soft, what day is this?
PARIS: Monday, my lord.
CAPULET: Monday? Ha, ha, well Wednesday is too soon;
A' Thursday let it be; a' Thursday, tell her
She shall be married to this noble earl. (III.iv.17)

And when Juliet seemingly agrees to the marriage, her father decides that it must be even sooner – Wednesday – 'I'll have this knot knit up tomorrow morning' (IV.ii.24). No chance to delay, 'we'll to church tomorrow' (IV.ii.37). Tomorrow comes, after a night of bustle, but all the preparations are vain. The bride is dead.

The speeding-up of Brooke's story not only shows the impetuosity of the lovers, but adds great poignancy to the play; they know that their first night together may well be their last. The plot seems to gather speed as it goes on, and the play moves faster and faster to its climax, till things are happening so quickly that the slightest slip may well cause disaster.

Finally, it is only by minutes that Romeo arrives too early at the tomb, and the Friar too late.

4 THEMES

4.1 CIVIL DISORDER

One theme, quite absent in Brooke, Shakespeare thought important enough to be brought in three times, at the beginning, the middle and the end of the play: the evil effects of civil strife. It was an Elizabethan commonplace that there was a 'great chain of being', from God through angels to men and down to the meanest creatures, 'which order God willeth us firmly to keep'. Their own world was far from orderly: civil war on the continent, rebellions and uprisings at home, war with Spain, rapid inflation, religious strife. But these were regarded as wrong, and (as Burgundy describes war-shattered France in *Henry V*) 'everything that seems unnatural'. God had planned an orderly universe with the earth in the centre, and the stars and the planets swinging round it in their appointed spheres. On earth the king, the nobility, the merchants and the various grades of ordinary people should move correspondingly in their appointed spheres, also in harmony.

> For government, though high and low and lower,
> Put into parts, doth keep in one consent,
> Congreeing in a full and natural close,
> Like music,

as Exeter reminds us in *Henry V* (I.ii.180).

For the political moral of *Romeo and Juliet* is the same as that of the English history plays, which Shakespeare was writing throughout the 1590s: if powerful individuals fight each other, the whole state and the ordinary citizens will suffer. In our play the city of Verona is plagued by continual disturbances in the streets; there is a long-standing feud between two powerful families, the Montagues and the Capulets, and members of the rival households cannot meet without brawling. Not till the quarrel has caused the death of the only children on either side will they make peace.

It is the most important duty of the ruler to preserve order, and this is a central concern. The opening scene of the play shows the feud checked for the time being by the authority of the prince; the central Act III shows the renewal of fighting bringing disaster; Act V shows the sacrifice of the innocents resulting in the end of the feud – too late. *Romeo and Juliet* ends with the Prince admitting his responsibility; by 'winking at their discords' (V.iii.293) and letting the feud continue, he has contributed to the disaster.

Order and disorder are contrasted, and so are their respective causes, love and hate. The word 'love', continually repeated, is found close to words such as 'rage' and rancour', and often to 'hate', throughout the play.

4.2 LOVE AND HATE

Everyone knows that *Romeo and Juliet* is a 'love story'. And how many and how various are the kinds of 'love' depicted in this play! Love to Old Capulet is just a minor addition to a marriage settlement; to the Nurse it is a mechanism for producing babies – one husband is as good as another. To Friar Lawrence love is a young man's weakness, that 'lies Not truly in their hearts, but in their eyes' (II.iii.67). The servants Samson and Gregory have a coarse physical ruthlessness; they will 'thrust. . .maids to the wall' (I.i.20) and take their maidenheads; to Mercutio too, love is lust: 'this drivelling love' he says, is like an idiot, 'like a great natural that runs lolling up and down to hide his bauble in a hole' (II.iv.97), and he mocks Romeo's early passion for Rosaline with much cynical bawdry. Shakespeare too makes fun of Romeo's affected, unreal adoration of Rosaline: had he actually met her? or simply adored from afar? Romeo is shown at first as a stock Elizabethan character, the 'melancholy lover', enchanted by a disdainful lady, sighing and weeping, shutting himself away from the world to mope alone, the Elizabethan descendant of the medieval courtly lover. But neither type of domination, by the masterful man nor by the tyrannical lady, leads to a really satisfactory relationship.

All these 'loves' are contrasted with the idyllic true love of Romeo and Juliet, true love of mind, body and spirit, each giving and each receiving.

Shakespeare also shows more than one aspect of love's opposite, hate, embodied in the fiery Tybalt and the icy Lady Capulet. The Elizabethans divided people roughly into four types, depending on which of the four 'humours' dominated in a man. He might be mainly choleric, sanguine, melancholy or phlegmatic. The ideal was to have equal quantities of each. Tybalt is not at all a complex personality, but is composed of pure choler, perpetually angry, looking for and causing trouble.

When Lady Capulet appears in I.iii she seems cold, almost indifferent, to her daughter, and describes Paris in a very formal and apparently emotionless passage (I.iii.81–94). But when Tybalt is killed, Lady Capulet does show emotion. She demands Romeo's death, then plans to send a man after the banished Romeo to poison him. She believes in 'an eye for an eye and a tooth for a tooth' and embodies the spirit of the feud.

4.3 THE 'GENERATION GAP'

Yet another theme is the 'generation gap', the sad misunderstanding of each other's feelings and motives by parents and children. Later, in *King Lear*, Shakespeare was to show these misunderstandings from the point of view of the old, but *Romeo and Juliet* is a play written by a youngish playwright about young people, and the story is told from their point of view. A city contains rival gangs; a girl from one side and a boy from the other fall in love, but have no chance of fulfilment and happiness. The play has been used as basis for the very successful musical set in modern New York, *West Side Story*. To bring it up to date we have only to replace 'Verona' in the first chorus by 'Belfast', where today it is impossible for a young Protestant to court a Catholic, and vice versa.

We see continual misunderstanding between Juliet and her parents, Juliet and her Nurse. Romeo's friend the Friar thinks he can influence Romeo's thoughts and actions by preaching to him, but the whole situation is summed up when Romeo utters the eternal cry of the young: 'Thou canst not speak of that thou dost not feel' (III.iii.64). The old have forgotten what it *felt* like to be young.

4.4 FORTUNE AND FATE

Brooke declares in his preliminary 'Address to the Reader' his intended moral. His 'unfortunate lovers', plagued by 'unhonest desire', neglecting the good advice of parents but taking the counsel of 'drunken gossips and superstitious friars', deserved their 'most unhappy death'. But actually in the poem itself he puts the blame on 'wavering Fortune's wheel', and Fortune is described as 'froward', 'tickle' [unstable], 'fierce', 'cruel', 'frayle unconstant' and 'full of change'.

The wheel of Fortune was a favourite medieval and Elizabethan image for the unreliability of man's life. Fortune, usually pictured as blindfolded, spun her wheel, and a man clinging to it might rise to its highest point; 'then Fortune in her shift and change of mood, Spurns down her late beloved *(Tcmon of Athens*, I.i.85); her wheel continued to spin, and down he came again.

To discover what his 'fortune' might be, an Elizabethan would consult an astrologer. The stars did not command, or even recommend, particular actions, but upon their positions there depended the outcome of whatever action was undertaken. For instance, Paris says he has not spoken of love to Juliet after her cousin's death, because 'Venus smiles not in a house of tears' (IV.i.8). That is, love-making does not go well with mourning, but also, the planet Venus, goddess of love, is not in a favourable 'house' in the heavens.

If the stars were unfavourable, then there would be disastrous happenings. We use the word today without realising that we are literally saying dis-astrous, ill-starred; when the Prologue announces that the lovers are 'star-crossed' (Prologue 6) the Elizabethan audience knows that they are doomed.

Yet the atmosphere of the first half of *Romeo and Juliet* is in many ways like that of one of Shakespeare's comedies. There are young lovers with tiresome parents, comic servants, fighting and masquing and jesting and dancing. The hero is a dreamy boy, with a much more practical girl – Romeo is meditating on the silver-sweetness of lovers' tongues while Juliet is asking, 'What o'clock tomorrow Shall I send to thee?' (II.ii.167). The relationship is like that of Bassanio and Portia in *The Merchant of Venice* or Orlando and Rosalind in *As You Like It*.

What makes the difference is the sense of unkind Fate or Fortune, of which the audience is continually reminded. In the Prologue the lovers are described not only as 'star-crossed', but also as 'misadventured', and their love is 'death-marked', marked for or by death. The critic Professor Mahood has pointed out that a 'mark' for Elizabethan seamen was a fixed point by which they steered, and that in several places the lovers' progress is compared to a voyage (I.v.112; II.ii.82; V.iii.117). Here then their 'passage' or voyage is towards death, and is 'fearful' in both meanings of the word – terrifying to experience and horrible to observe. Even on the way to the Capulet feast Romeo feels "tis no wit to go' (I.iv.49) and his 'mind misgives Some consequence yet hanging in the stars', which will lead to his 'untimely death' (I.iv.106,111). Tybalt too forecasts that Romeo's 'seeming-sweet' escapade at the feast will turn to 'bitterest gall' (I.v.91). Even at his wedding Romeo envisages and defies 'love-devouring death' (II.vi.7), and when Mercutio is slain he foresees a train of disasters: 'This but begins the woe others must end' (III.i.124). Romeo does not blame his own clumsy intervention for Mercutio's death and, when he kills Tybalt, blames Fortune: 'O I am fortune's fool!' (III.i.140). Friar Lawrence seems correct in describing Romeo as *'wedded* to calamity' – bound with a life-long inescapable tie (III.iii.3).

When Romeo hears of Juliet's supposed death, he cries, 'Then I defy you stars' (V.i.24), and dashes off to Verona to kill himself, as being the only way to escape from the 'yoke of inauspicious stars' which has been so literally dis-astrous. (V.3.111).

Even at first sight of Juliet Romeo thinks her beauty is 'too rich for use, for earth too dear' (I.v.48) and when each discovers the other's identity another note of apprehension is struck. Juliet declares the birth of her love to be 'prodigious' (I.v.141), that is, monstrous or deformed, and a 'prodigious' birth (say of a two-headed calf or a six-fingered child) was thought to be an extremely bad omen. Even in the bliss of the orchard a chill note is struck when Juliet declares that their love is

> . . .too rash, too unadvised, too sudden,
> Too like the lightning, which doth cease to be
> Ere one can say 'It lightens'.   (II.ii.118)

As disaster follows disaster Juliet grieves that 'heaven should practise stratagems Upon so soft a subject as myself' (III.v.209). Again and again she unwittingly forecasts future horrors. When parting from Romeo her 'ill-divining soul' makes her imagine him 'as one dead in the bottom of a tomb' (III.v.54, 56) and it is so indeed that she next sees him. She rightly foresees her 'bridal bed' being made 'in that dim monument where Tybalt lies' (III.v.201) and rather than marry Paris she says she will – and later does – hide herself 'in a charnel house, O'er-covered quite with dead men's rattling bones' (IV.i.81).

All these horrors are made to seem inevitable. 'The heavens do lour upon you for some ill' (IV.v.94) says Friar Lawrence, and 'A greater power than we can contradict Hath thwarted our intents' (V.3.153). The Prince declares that 'heaven finds means to kill your joys with love' – the love of the Montague and Capulet children has brought not happiness but tragedy.

4.5 IS THE PLAY A TRAGEDY?

Some critics have said that *Romeo and Juliet* cannot be called a tragedy, because the disaster is caused only by a series of unfortunate accidents – Friar John being prevented from letting Romeo know that Juliet was really still alive, Romeo knowing where to get poison at a moment's notice, Romeo arriving at the tomb before the Friar, and Juliet waking a few moments too late – instead of by some weakness in the character of the hero. H. B. Charlton writes that 'as a pattern of the idea of tragedy [*Romeo and Juliet*] is a failure'. But Shakespeare did not write the play to be dissected by scholars 'as a pattern of the idea of tragedy'. He wrote it to waken in the audience in the theatre tragic feelings of sacrifice, waste and desolation. And in this he succeeded. All Elizabethan editions of the play class it as a tragedy, and Dr Samuel Johnson (1709–84), great eighteenth-century critic and editor of Shakespeare, the least sentimental of men, thought that the catastrophe was 'irresistibly affecting'.

Friar Lawrence on his first appearance tells us that there is a struggle in man between 'grace and rude will', and if the latter triumphs, 'full soon the canker death eats up that plant' (II.iii.30). This is a constant theme in Shakespeare's later tragedies. Antony perishes because he makes 'his will' (that is, desire, passionate impulse) 'lord of his reason' (*Antony and Cleopatra*, III.xiii.3). Hamlet praises Horatio because he is not 'passion's slave' (III.ii.77). But Romeo is indeed 'passion's slave'. He never pauses to think what the consequences of his actions may be: all that matters is the emotion of the moment, not its duration but its intensity. He has no use for the Friar's caution: 'Wisely and slow, they stumble that run fast' (II.iii.94). Surely there is bitter irony in the fact that if the Friar had hurried to the tomb, when he heard that his message had miscarried, he might have prevented the catastrophe.

Such speculations are irrelevant. We have known from the beginning that the play precisely illustrates Thomas Hardy's definition of tragedy: 'the worthy encompassed by the inevitable'.

5 SUMMARY AND COMMENTARY

Prologue

The noisy audience was probably called to attention by a trumpet call. Then an actor entered as the 'Chorus'. He was an observer, not a character in the play, so was free to comment to the audience on what was about to happen. His task was to 'put them in the picture', and he recited a sonnet, a popular form of verse at the time (see page 73).

We are in northern Italy, in Verona, a town continually disturbed by a long-standing feud between two important families. A boy from one family falls in love with a girl from the other, and after a series of accidents, both die. At last, too late, the parents come to their senses and make peace.

The play, says the Chorus, will take some two hours. There were no intervals in Elizabethan public theatres, but even so the version presented must have been considerably shorter than the one we have now – perhaps the first Quarto.

Act I

Summary

Shakespeare immediately introduces us to a scene of gang warfare between Capulets and Montagues (probably like the brawls in the streets of his London between Sir Walter Ralegh's men and those of the Earl of Essex). It begins with the servants of each house and quickly spreads until even the aged heads of the two families are brawling. The prince silences the tumult, and threatens future offenders with death. We meet the moping lover Romeo, a Montague, and hear him complaining to his friend Benvolio of his lady Rosaline's hard-heartedness.

Capulet interviews Paris, a suitor for his daughter Juliet, and invites Paris to a feast in his house that night. Benvolio and Romeo learn that Rosaline will be at the feast, and decide to attend it, uninvited.

Next we meet Lady Capulet, breaking the news of Paris's wooing to her daughter Juliet – news that excites Juliet's Nurse, a trusted family servant.

Romeo and his friends, including Mercutio, go to the feast disguised as masquers, and are welcomed by old Capulet. But the 'fiery Tybalt' recognises Romeo as a Montague and wishes to fight him. Old Capulet will not have fighting under his roof, so Tybalt leaves, uttering threats. Meanwhile Romeo has caught sight of Juliet, and has completely forgotten Rosaline. They meet, speak and kiss; but when later each discovers the other's identity, they realise that the feud makes an almost impassable barrier between them.

Act I, scene i

Two Capulet servants begin the play with some obvious puns and coarse jokes against the Montagues; meeting two Montague servants, they first insult them and, when they see support arriving in the form of a young Capulet gallant, Tybalt, challenge them. Benvolio, a Montague (and as well-wishing as his name implies) tries to keep the peace; but Tybalt, fiercest of Capulets, forces Benvolio to fight, and soon the stage is a flurry of skirmishing figures, joined finally by old Capulet and old Montague, whose wives struggle to restrain them. The citizens who come running in do not take sides, but, tired of this disruptive behaviour, shout impartially 'Down with the Capulets! Down with the Montagues!' (76)

Shakespeare, having thus captured the attention of his audience and given them a lively picture of the state of the feud, now silences the tumult by bringing on the Prince, rightly furious with both families. He rebukes them in elaborate stately language, in a long speech contrasting sharply with the hurried one- or two-line speeches up to this point.

> Rebellious subjects, enemies to peace,
> Profaners of this neighbour-stained steel. . .
> On pain of torture, from those bloody hands
> Throw your mistempered weapons to the ground. . . (93,98)

Some critics refuse to take the feud seriously, but the Prince speaks with great gravity and severity. He says that this is the third riot caused by the 'cankered hate' of the families, and that it must be the last. If there is any more street fighting, the culprits will be put to death.

Montague and his wife are left with Benvolio, who tells them how the fray began, emphasising the 'fiery Tybalt's' part, who had appeared with 'his sword prepared'. The situation is established, so now Lady Montague asks where her son, Romeo, is, and Benvolio and Montague break into yet another contrasting manner of speech. The 'melancholy lover' was in the

1590s a stock Elizabethan character, already sketched by Shakespeare in *Two Gentlemen of Verona*: 'You have learnt. . . to walk alone, like one that had the pestilence; to sigh, like a schoolboy that had lost his ABC; to weep, like a young wench that had buried her grandma; to fast. . .to watch, like one that fears robbing; to speak puling' (II.i.18). Romeo too shuns company, weeps and sighs, wanders at night and shuts himself up in his room all day, continually bemoaning from afar the stony heart of his lady. This is the picture they draw, and when Romeo appears he acts up to it. But how seriously?

After a few lines of love poetry he breaks off to ask 'Where shall we dine?' (175) and then, noticing signs of the fighting – perhaps abandoned weapons – shows his weariness of the feud.

> O me, what fray was here?
> Yet tell me not, for I have heard it all. (175)

Now he contrasts love and hate (a major theme of the play) and throws off a series of fantastic comparisons of opposites,

> O heavy lightness, serious vanity. . .
> Feather of lead, bright smoke, cold fire, sick health (180)

surely another sign that this is hardly an expression of deep feeling, but rather of fashionable affectation. Like Armado in *Love's Labour's Lost*, Romeo

> hath a mint of phrases in his brain;
> One whom the music of his own vain tongue
> Doth ravish like enchanting harmony. (I.i.164)

After more elegant versifying – 'Love is a smoke made with a fume of sighs' (192) and another line or two, Romeo runs out of comparisons, but saying 'What is it else?' (195) while he thinks, he recovers and adds a few more. Benvolio begs him to be serious: 'Tell me, in sadness' (that is, truly) 'who is that you love?' (201) But Romeo still teases: 'In sadness, cousin, I do love – a woman' (206). And he goes on to describe her in the language of formal love-poetry, using images of love as war, and love as religion: 'Cupid's arrow', 'siege', 'encounter', 'saint-seducing gold'. He bewails her sworn chastity, and refuses Benvolio's advice to 'examine other beauties' (230).

The impression given is of a very young man in love, not with a lady, but with the idea of being in love. Later the impression is given that Romeo is younger than Benvolio and Mercutio; perhaps he feels that he too must have a mistress, even if only in imagination.

So far the play has proceeded by a series of contrasting episodes: the crude lust and anger of Samson and Gregory; the disorderly fight; the judgement of the Prince; the romantic introduction of the hero, so affectedly lovelorn. In the next scene 'love' will be seen in a quite different context, as an adjunct to a financial settlement.

Act I, scene ii

The Count Paris, young, handsome and a kinsman of the Prince, is asking for the hand of Capulet's daughter, Juliet. But first Shakespeare rouses our hopes of an ending to the feud by having old Capulet say that perhaps it *is* time for 'men so old' as himself and Montague to keep the peace. He tells Paris that Juliet is not quite fourteen, but that if Paris can 'get her heart', then Capulet will give his consent to the match. Juliet is his only child, 'Earth [the grave] hath swallowed all my hopes but she', and therefore she is a rich heiress, 'She is the hopeful lady of my earth [property]'. (*'Fille de terre'* means heiress).

It is obvious that Capulet's concern is that she will make a good match in the worldly sense, and that he has no doubt that his daughter will obey him in everything. Shakespeare introduces the rival suitor Paris before Romeo and Juliet have even seen one another, so that when they do meet we already know of Capulet's far different plans for her future.

Capulet invites Paris to a feast that night in the Capulet mansion, and gives a servant a list of the guests to be invited. The illiterate servant meets Romeo (still arguing with Benvolio about love) and asks him to read the list of names aloud. Among the names Romeo reads 'My fair niece Rosaline', which must be strongly emphasised. Benvolio suggests that if they go to the feast he can show Romeo many ladies much fairer than Rosaline:

> Compare her face with some that I shall show,
> And I will make thee think thy swan a crow.   (87)

Romeo, in a formal stanza of love-poetry, says that this is impossible:

> When the devout religion of mine eye
>   Maintains such falsehood, then turn tears to fires,
> And those who, often drowned, could never die,
>   Transparent heretics, be burnt for liars.

These elaborate lines – far too elaborate for a theatre audience to grasp at first hearing – suggest that here Shakespeare is writing simply for his own pleasure in poetry rather than for the listener. Romeo declares that his eyes are worshippers, adoring his mistress as the most beautiful of all women, and would be heretics if they admitted that anyone excelled her. Then his tears, which have often drenched, but not drowned, his eyes, would turn to fires, and, just as heretics were burned, destroy his false-believing eyes. And in case the audience have not followed all this, two crystal-clear lines follow:

> One fairer than my love? The all-seeing sun
> Ne'er saw her match since first the world begun.   (93)

Nevertheless, he will not lose a chance of seeing Rosaline, and agrees to gate crash the Capulet feast.

Act I, scene iii

We are now taken into the Capulet house to meet Juliet, her mother and her Nurse. Juliet appears to be a quiet, docile child, attending her mother's summons: 'Madam, I am here. What is your will?' (6) Lady Capulet wishes to tell Juliet about the proposed marriage to Paris, but can hardly get a word in edgeways, since the Nurse babbles on unendingly. When asked to confirm Juliet's age, she calculates at great length that it is eleven years since Juliet was weaned, on a day when an earthquake shook the dovehouse, with many other irrelevant particulars. At length we learn that Juliet is fourteen, but on goes the Nurse, with an anecdote of her husband picking up the baby Juliet, who had fallen on her face.

> 'Yea,' quoth he, 'dost thou fall upon thy face?
> Thou wilt fall backward when thou hast more wit,
> Wilt thou not, Jule?' And by my holidame,
> The pretty wretch left crying, and said 'Ay.'   (41)

This mildly indecent jest so pleases the nurse that despite Lady Capulet's displeasure she repeats it three times. Her rambling, repetitive speech, hearty and irrepressible, establishes her as a robust, unsubtle character, delighted at the prospect of Juliet's marriage and jumping forward at once to the idea of pregnancy with Juliet growing 'bigger; women grow by men'. (95)

The poet, Samuel Taylor Coleridge (1772–1834) considers it 'characteristic of the ignorance of the Nurse' that 'in all her recollections she assists herself by the remembrance of visual circumstances. . . the cultivated mind will be found to recall the past by certain regular trains of cause and effect; whereas, with the uncultivated mind, the past is recalled wholly by coincident images or facts that happened at the same time.' He could hardly have found a better illustration than the Nurse's long speech.

Juliet on the contrary hardly speaks at all. Marriage is to her 'an honour that I dream not of' (66) but she will do as she is bidden. The Elizabethans imagined that love might arise when two people 'exchanged eyes', and that 'fancy', love at first sight, was 'engendered in the eyes' (*Merchant of Venice*, III.ii.67). So Juliet says, meekly but wittily, 'I'll look to like, if looking liking move' (97), that is, 'I'll gaze at Paris, in order to love him, if it is indeed true that looking at someone makes you love him.' In fact, it will be Romeo with whom she will 'exchange eyes', and Paris will be quite forgotton. But meanwhile Juliet seems prepared to obey her parents implicitly:

> But no more deep will I endart mine eye
> Than your consent gives strength to make it fly. (98)

Lady Capulet, like any well-to-do Elizabethan, takes it for granted that marriage has nothing to do with falling in love. Juliet is the sole heir of the 'great rich Capulet' (I.ii.80) and her marriage is an affair of parental negotiation, not of personal inclination.

Juliet and her mother are summoned to the feast; the Nurse watches them go off, already foreseeing the 'happy nights' of Juliet's marriage.

Act I, scene iv

It was not unusual in the sixteenth century for small masked groups in fancy dress to turn up uninvited at a feast or gathering, to recite or perform some masque or dance. Shakespeare had already shown this happening in *Love's Labour's Lost*. The king and his friends disguise themselves as Russians, introduced by the page Moth, stumbling over his ill-learnt prologue. They entertain the Princess and her ladies, who pretend not to recognise them, and so can speak to them freely, without courtly etiquette. Romeo and his friends form just such a group, and discuss whether it is necessary to announce themselves by a preliminary speech. Benvolio decides that 'no without-book prologue, faintly spoke After the prompter' (7) is necessary:

> . . .let them measure us by what they will,
> We'll measure them a measure and be gone.   (9)

Never mind what their standards are, he says, we'll allow them just a dance, and then leave. Such word-play, using the same word in different senses, was an admired Elizabethan skill, and the young men in the play continually show their wit by this kind of punning (see page 70).

Romeo seems moody and miserable, though it does not prevent him from joining in the word-play. He refuses to dance, will only carry a torch: 'Being but heavy [miserable] I will bear the light'. For dancing one needs 'nimble soles' on one's shoes, but he says he has 'a soul of lead'. Mercutio joins in and they explore many meanings of, for instance, 'bound', 'done' and 'dun', 'sore' and 'soar'.

Romeo, however, is full of misgivings about the whole enterprise. He refuses to take part: 'I'll be a candle-holder and look on' (38) for "tis no wit to go'. He begins to tell of an ominous dream he has had, but Mercutio will not listen and bursts out with one of the best-known of Shakespeare's set pieces, the 'Queen Mab' speech. It has been suggested that the actor who played Mercutio, knowing that he was to die in Act III and (since there were no curtain calls in Elizabethan playhouses) would never be seen again by the audience, demanded at least one substantial solo speech. Be that as it may, this speech lets Mercutio dominate the stage for a considerable time.

The opening passage about Mab's coach may be pretty and quaint, but soon Mercutio's satirical wit takes over, and he presents a cynical view of society. Courtiers bow and scrape, lawyers care only for fees, ladies' breath is abhorrent because they eat too many sweetmeats. (In Elizabethan days, without dentistry, foreign ambassadors did complain of the black teeth and bad breath of the ladies at the English court.) When Queen Mab becomes a 'hag', a malignant sprite, who leans on maidens to accustom them to bearing the weight of their lovers, and to bearing children, Romeo interrupts, but Mercutio cannot be stopped. He does change his tune though, breaking into serious poetry:

> I talk of dreams
> Which are the children of an idle brain,
> Begot of nothing but vain fantasy,
> Which is as thin of substance as the air,
> And more inconstant than the wind who woos
> Even now the frozen bosom of the north,
> And being angered puffs away from thence,
> Turning his side to the dew-dropping south.   (96)

It is like an unwitting forecast of the inconstant Romeo's turn from the icy Rosaline to the warm, welcoming Juliet.

Romeo still hangs back. In one of many premonitions of evil his

> mind misgives
> Some consequence, yet hanging in the stars,
> Shall bitterly begin his fearful date
> With this night's revels.   (106)

He even foresees his own 'untimely death' (111). But urged by his friends he goes in, with them, to the feast.

Act I, scene v

All is bustle in the Capulet mansion. Servants are clearing the feast away, and Capulet, among his guests, welcomes the masquers. He recalls his own dancing days, thirty years before: 'I have seen the day That I have worn a visor'. But now "Tis gone, 'tis gone, 'tis gone'. He returns to his present function as host: 'You are welcome, gentlemen' (23). Capulet does not resent the uninvited intruders, on the contrary he says 'this unlooked for sport comes well' (31).

Romeo has not joined the dancers, but has been enchanted by his first sight of Juliet. He asks a servingman her name, but the man is not of the household, and does not know it. At once Romeo conceives Juliet's beauty as flaming or flickering light seen against darkness:

> O she doth teach the torches to burn bright.
> It seems she hangs upon the cheek of night
> As a rich jewel in an Ethiop's ear.   (45)

The two lovers will picture each other thus throughout the play, as sparks of light against the surrounding dark.

Despite Romeo's mask, Tybalt has recognised him as a Montague, and immediately calls for his rapier: 'To strike him dead I hold it not a sin' (60). Old Capulet has no intention of allowing the feud to break out again so soon, especially under his own roof. He has already said that he and Montague should now contrive to 'keep the peace' (I.ii.3) and now he acknowledges that Romeo is thought to be 'a virtuous and well-governed youth' (69). He bids Tybalt be patient – an impossibility – and while the dancing goes on Old Capulet (himself short-tempered) and Tybalt have a sharp quarrel. Old Capulet tries at the same time to control Tybalt, to encourage the dancers and to call to the servants for more lights. Tybalt is over-ruled, but leaves in a rage, making a grim forecast that 'this intrusion shall Now seeming sweet, convert to bitterest gall' (92).

Meanwhile the dance has brought Juliet to where Romeo is standing; ignoring all else, they are absorbed in one another. If Romeo had been one of the invited guests, it would have been against every rule of conduct that he should speak of love, in his own person, to a daughter of the house whom he had just seen for the first time. But masquers were allowed liberties, and he could express his real feelings under the pretence of play-acting, as a pilgrim approaching a saint. If he is disguised as a palmer, or pilgrim (and 'romeo' is the Italian word for pilgrim) then he is talking in character, though both he and Juliet feel the real underlying sincerity of what he is saying. He is not (as he was before) solely concerned with his own state of mind, but with a mutual exchange.

They speak a sonnet, a formal poem of fourteen lines (see page 73). At first sight they have 'exchanged eyes', and are deeply moved. Romeo takes Juliet's hand as a pilgrim might a relic, and seeks permission to kiss it.

> If I profane with my unworthiest hand
> This holy shrine, the gentle sin is this,
> My lips, two blushing pilgrims, ready stand
> To smooth that rough touch with a tender kiss.   (94)

Modest Juliet neither accepts nor refuses. She responds by saying that 'palm to palm is holy palmers' kiss' – if he is a pilgrim, then let his hands meet as for prayer. Romeo argues that both saints and palmers have lips – yes, says Juliet, to be used in praying. Romeo, still speaking as a pilgrim at a shrine, but getting more and more intense, calls her 'dear saint' and says that his lips *are* praying – for a kiss. Juliet argues that the statues of saints may grant prayers, but do not move, and Romeo takes this as permission to move himself, and to kiss her, and so the sonnet ends. But at once he starts again; she is a saint who has taken away his sin. Perhaps this exchange has been sweetly-solemn long enough, for surely Juliet smiles as she says that then her lips must have 'the sin that they have took'. Romeo leaps at the opportunity to ask if he may kiss her again, to take back the sin. And Juliet teases him: 'You kiss by the book' (111) – that is, you don't kiss until you have justified it by explanation.

Their privacy is too good to last. Suddenly the Nurse calls Juliet away, and Romeo discovers that he has fallen hopelessly, completely, utterly in love with the daughter of his greatest enemy. 'O dear account' he cries, 'dear' being both 'cherished' and 'expensive', 'my life is my foe's debt'.

Old Capulet hospitably urges the masquers to stay and take some refreshment, but they withdraw. Juliet, in order to discover Romeo's identity, artfully asks her Nurse to name *all* the young men as they go out. With unconscious prophesy she fears that if Romeo is married, and not free to marry her, 'my grave is like to be my wedding-bed'. When she discovers that he is a Montague, she dreads that her new love is a 'prodigious birth', ill-omened. After the touching meeting of the lovers, and their delight in one another, their happiness is immediately shattered, because of the feud.

Shakespeare never merely *tells* us what is going on. He *shows* us an image of the feud in action, on the street and at the feast. And the love shown by Romeo and Juliet is contrasted with the hatred of the raging Tybalt.

Act II: Chorus

In some versions of the play the Chorus appears again at this point, but his verses are generally cut in performance. He only tells the audience what they already know – that Romeo's fancy has left Rosaline and lighted on Juliet, 'bewitched by the charm of looks' (6), more importantly, perhaps, that instead of languishing hopelessly he 'is beloved and loves again' (5). But they are parted by their families' enmity. Nevertheless the chorus promises that the strength of their passion will somehow enable them to meet.

Act II

Summary
Leaving the Capulet feast, Romeo slips away from Benvolio and Mercutio
and climbs a wall into the Capulet orchard. Juliet comes out on her balcony
above and muses aloud on her love for Romeo, and her misery because he
is a Montague. He shows himself, and they exchange vows of love. Juliet
is willing to marry Romeo immediately – no other relationship is envisaged
– and arranges to send a messenger to Romeo next morning, to discover
what plans he has made for their union. Romeo goes straight to his confessor, Friar Lawrence, who agrees to marry them at once.

Next day we see Romeo, now in the highest spirits, fooling with his
friends, and arranging with the Nurse that Juliet should go, under pretence
of confession, to Friar Lawrence's cell. As soon as she receives the message
Juliet hastens to the cell, and without more ado Friar Lawrence marries
them.

Act II, scenes i and ii

These scenes are continuous – the division was made by an eighteenth-
century editor to suit the conventions of that period.

The action too is really continuous from I.v, because we see Romeo
going home from the feast, but, reluctant to go further from Juliet, turning
back towards the Capulet house, where (he says) his heart still is. Benvolio
and Mercutio come past, trying to overtake Romeo, to tease him about his
lovelorn state, still, they think, caused by Rosaline. Mercutio, bursting
with high spirits, pretends to be a conjuror or magician, and utters a mock
spell, full of sexual innuendo, conjuring by Rosaline's 'quivering thigh,
And the desmenes [estates] that there adjacent lie' (II.i.19). Benvolio, as
usual, tries to quieten him, but there is no restraining Mercutio, and he
proceeds from one outrageous indecency to another. When, unable to discover Romeo, Mercutio and Benvolio break off to go home, Romeo emerges
from hiding; he dismisses them and Mercutio's bawdiness, in one line: 'He
jests at scars that never felt a wound' (II.ii.1) – the man who has never
been wounded by love cannot understand its pains.

Now Shakespeare in his Elizabethan theatre, in daylight and with no
artificial lighting save torches, must create a cool moonlit scene (see page 67)
in which the pure flame of the lovers' devotion comes as an extreme contrast to the atmosphere of heat and 'rank sweat' (as Shakespeare describes
it in *Hamlet*, III.iv.92) engendered by Mercutio's bawdry.

Juliet comes out on her balcony, above Romeo, as if she were indeed
'for earth too dear' (I.v.48) or one of Capulet's 'earth-treading stars that
make dark heaven light' (I.ii.25). Shakespeare places Romeo below, looking
up at her, thus seemingly inevitably his words and comparisons lead up-

wards: arise – sun, moon, stars, heaven, spheres, bright angel – and are
light-giving: light, twinkle, brightness, daylight, lamp – or are floating above
in the 'airy region': birds, winged messenger of heaven, lazy puffing clouds
all sailing upon the bosom of the air. Romeo's loving praises are no longer
formally fantastic. Juliet is, conventionally enough, 'the sun' – the sun is
powerful enough to outshine the moon, symbol of virgin chastity and
perhaps of Rosaline, and of 'green-sickness', which was pallor and anaemia
in young girls, caused, said the Elizabethans, by 'want of a husband'. But
how direct and simple Romeo can now be:

> It is my lady, O it is my love.
> O that she knew she were.   (10)

Juliet, thinking herself alone, confesses her love and laments the feud.
The meek little girl has been transformed. For Romeo she will abandon
her family:

> Be but sworn my love
> And I'll no longer be a Capulet. . .
> What's in a name? . . .Romeo doff thy name,
> And for that name which is no part of thee,
> Take all myself.   (35, 43, 47)

The delighted Romeo can no longer be silent, and calls out, 'I take thee at
thy word' (49). Juliet is naturally terrified to think that some stranger
is lurking below her window, but Romeo reassures her with, as it were, a
recognition signal, calling her 'dear saint', as he did at the ball. But now
she finds a new cause for alarm; it is death to a Montague to be found in
Capulet's garden, and though Romeo brushes this aside – their hate is
nothing if he has her love – Juliet has next a more private and personal
cause for embarrassment. Against all convention, all the rules of her up-
bringing, she has, unasked, confessed her love, and Romeo has overheard
her. Only 'the mask of night' (85) affords some shelter, as Romeo's mask
had when first they met.

Juliet has been brought up to 'dwell on form' (88), to behave in a re-
strained, conventional way, but what of that? 'Farewell compliment' (89),
she says, goodbye to etiquette. If he is still conventional enough to think
her surrender too abrupt, she is willing to 'frown and be perverse, and say
thee nay. . .but else, not for the world' (96). With the utmost sincerity
and simplicity she promises, 'I'll prove more true Than those that have
more cunning to be strange' (100). Light and darkness are again contrasted;
it is not 'light love' (wanton behaviour) that the 'dark night' has disclosed.

Romeo too has neglected 'form' by eavesdropping and overhearing
Juliet's soliloquy, and still more by declaring his love directly to Juliet,
instead of, like Paris, approaching her father. Juliet will not let him swear

his love by 'th'unconstant', ever-changing moon, and does not wish him to swear at all. A chill comes over her. She realises that their love is 'too rash, too unadvised, too sudden' (118) and – again a brief flashing light against the dark – 'too like the lightning, which doth cease to be Ere one can say, "It lightens".' (119) It is an ominous comparison. At the opposite extreme from Sampson and Mercutio, Juliet's love is not all-taking, but all-giving.

> My bounty is as boundless as the sea
> My love as deep; the more I give to thee
> The more I have, for both are infinite.   (133)

The Nurse calls Juliet in, and Romeo, left alone, cannot believe that he has indeed exchanged vows with his love. He is lost in a happy dream when Juliet returns and promises to marry him as soon as he can arrange it. They cannot bear to part. She returns again, with a very practical question as to when she should send her messenger to him in the morning, and Shakespeare achieves that rarest of literary successes, a lovers' dialogue which is lifelike and yet neither silly nor sloppy when overheard by a third party. T. S. Eliot's comment on the poetry of the balcony scene seems applicable here: 'In this scene Shakespeare achieves a perfection of verse...which neither he nor anyone else could excel – for this particular purpose.'

JULIET: I have forgot why I did call thee back.
ROMEO: Let me stand here till thou remember it.
JULIET: I shall forget, to have thee still stand there
Rememb'ring how I love thy company.
ROMEO: And I'll still stay, to have thee still forget,
Forgetting any other home but this...
JULIET: Good-night, good-night. Parting is such sweet sorrow
That I shall say 'Good night' till it be morrow.   (170)

Romeo, determined on immediate marriage, hastens off to his confessor, Friar Lawrence.

Act II, scene iii
The sheer emotion of scene ii is followed by the cool rationality of Friar Lawrence. Brooke describes his friar:

> The secrets eke he knew in Nature's works that lurk;
> By magic's art most men supposed that he could wonders work.

Shakespeare accepts this description and first presents Friar Lawrence in the dawn, gathering herbs for medicine, thus preparing us for his production of the 'magic' potion later in the play. He is also moralising. All plants, he says, contain both good and bad qualities, depending on how they are used; the same thing applies to men. God has given man 'rude will' (28), that is, desire, impulse, passion (often with sexual overtones), qualities which man shares with the beasts. 'Grace', which here includes reason and judgement, God gives to man alone, so that he can direct and control his animal passions, which are not evil in themselves, but useful if rightly directed. We may see Romeo as the embodiment of unreflecting passionate impulse, and the Friar as exemplifying 'grace' and reason, which are not in this case strong enough to control Romeo's 'rude will'.

The Friar's long-winded enquiries eventually draw from Romeo a plain statement of his desire: to be married immediately to Capulet's daughter. The astonished Friar, remembering Romeo's tears, sighs and groans for Rosaline, accuses him of inconstancy:

> Lo here upon thy cheek the stain doth sit
> Of an old tear that is not washed off yet.   (75)

The Friar (surely irresponsibly) requires little or no persuasion to fall in with Romeo's plan, remarking with unconscious irony that this marriage may turn the hate between the families to 'pure love' – yet again we have the juxtaposition of these qualities. Romeo is full of 'sudden haste' and the Friar does nothing to restrain him, content merely to remark, 'Wisely and slow. They stumble that run fast' (94).

Act II, scene iv

Meanwhile Mercutio and Benvolio wonder what has happened to Romeo. They know that Tybalt has sent a letter of challenge to Montague's house. But, says Mercutio, since Romeo is already dead of love, 'stabbed with a white wench's black eye' (15), how can a dead man fight Tybalt, who is one of those most skilled in the new fashion of duelling, fighting rhythmically as if to music.

But when Romeo joins them, he is far from dead. He is utterly changed from the dismal youth of the previous evening. He is in the highest spirits, and joins in a battle of wits and nonsensical word-play, causing Mercutio to rejoice: 'Why, is not this better than groaning for love? Now art thou sociable, now art thou Romeo...'. Mercutio scorns 'this drivelling love', this babbling, slavering love, an idiot with his tongue hanging out, who only seeks physical relief for his lust. Mercutio has no idea how far removed this picture is from Romeo's love.

Frequently Shakespeare contrives to include his stage directions in his text, and so require the actor to move or even dress in a particular way. When the Nurse enters to cries of 'Here's goodly gear! A sail, a sail!' (108)

she must come billowing on to the stage like a full-rigged ship. Her arrival leads to more jesting – though Romeo ominously describes Mercutio as one 'that God hath made for himself to mar' – and some horseplay. The Nurse seems garrulous as ever, and good-natured enough, warning Romeo not to lead Juliet into 'a fool's paradise' (173). She willingly agrees to tell Juliet to come to Friar Lawrence's cell that very afternoon.

This scene has a different flavour from those immediately before it, because Shakespeare has the young men talk, not in the flowing rhythms of poetry, but in a lively prose, 'full of snappy wisecracks'.

Act II, scene v

The Nurse had left the Capulet house at nine o'clock. Now it is noon, and Juliet has been waiting anxiously for 'three long hours' (11), bitterly contrasting the swiftness of youth with the slowness of age – 'old folks. . . Unwieldy, slow, heavy and pale as lead'.

At last the Nurse comes, but to Juliet's eager enquiries she merely complains of her own weariness and breathlessness, and though she praises Romeo, she says nothing to the point. Indeed she must be grossly insensitive, or else inclined to painfully mischievous teasing, when to Juliet's persistent coaxing – 'Sweet, sweet, sweet nurse, tell me what says my love?' (55) she pretends to answer, but breaks off at the critical moment: 'Your love says, like an honest gentlemen, and a courteous, and a kind, and a handsome, and I warrant a virtuous – Where is your mother?' (56). And Juliet has to endure more complaining before at last she hears the message:

> . . .hie you hence to Friar Lawrence' cell;
> There stays a husband to make you a wife.   (69)

The Nurse will fetch a ladder by which Romeo can climb to Juliet's balcony, and adds heartily,

> I am the drudge, and toil in your delight,
> But you shall bear the burden soon at night,   (76)

while Juliet, ironically hailing 'high fortune', hurries off to her wedding.

Act II, scene vi

At the cell, Romeo and Friar Lawrence are waiting for Juliet, the Friar apparently a little nervous, in case 'after-hours' bring 'sorrow'. Romeo however is exalted; he brushes aside doubt and challenges fortune:

> Do thou but close our hands with holy words,
> Then love-devouring death do what he dare,
> It is enough I may but call her mine.   (6)

Lawrence, though rashly willing to wed them secretly, is full of wise words:

'These violent delights have violent ends', he says, and warns that 'fire and powder. . .as they kiss, consume'. The use of the word 'kiss' rather than 'meet' or 'touch' brings home the comparison to the lovers; 'Consume' means both 'reach consummation' and 'die by being burnt away'. 'Love moderately' (14) says the Friar, but Romeo is deaf to such elderly wisdom, and again the gap between the generations is emphasised.

When Juliet arrives there is a short but intense exchange of greetings between the lovers.

ROMEO: Ah, Juliet, if the measure of thy joy
        Be heaped like mine. . .
        . . .then sweeten with thy breath
        This neighbour air, and let rich music's tongue
        Unfold the imagined happiness that both
        Receive in either by this dear encounter.   (24)

Shakespeare plays with words here by linking them in different groups. Romeo's joy is like a heaped-up overflowing 'measure' (a portion or allowance of corn), but a 'measure' is also a song which will *sweeten* the air, and '*rich* music' will convey the happiness of this '*dear*' (both beloved and valuable) '*encounter*'.

Juliet responds in the same strain. Only beggars can '*count* their *worth*'. Juliet's overflowing 'excess' of love cannot be measured: 'I cannot *sum* up *sum* of half my *wealth*'.

This is a curious anticipation of another of Shakespeare's lovers who was ruined by love; Antony's opening words in *Antony and Cleopatra* are 'There's beggary in the love that can be reckoned'. Both Juliet and Antony give unlimited love, and in the end this kills them.

Of course the audience in the theatre cannot work out these relationships as the words are said, but the effect is one of great richness and complexity, and seems to echo Romeo's first assessment of Juliet's 'beauty too *rich* for *use*, for *earth* too *dear*' (I.v.48), with its multiple meanings. The critic Professor Mahood has pointed out that 'use' is both 'employment' and 'interest', from 'usury'; 'earth' is both 'mortal life' and 'the grave'; 'dear' is both 'beloved' and 'expensive'.

The Friar, apparently forgetting his doubts, and with no more hesitation, leads them off to be married.

Act III

Summary

Mercuţio and Benvolio, wandering through the streets in the hot summer afternoon, encounter Tybalt, and exchange jeers. But Tybalt is really looking for Romeo, to challenge him for gate crashing the Capulet feast.

Romeo refuses to fight his new cousin-by-marriage; Mercutio is shocked by this apparent cowardice, and fights Tybalt himself. Romeo endeavours to come between them, which enables Tybalt to wound Mercutio fatally. Mercutio dies, cursing both the feuding houses. Romeo, burning with shame, fights and kills Tybalt.

Furious citizens, the angry Prince and members of both households crowd the stage. Lady Capulet demands Romeo's death, in revenge, and the Prince banishes Romeo from Verona.

Juliet appears on her balcony, oblivious of what has happened, longing for night and the coming of her bridegroom. Instead the weeping nurse brings her the news of Tybalt's death and Romeo's banishment.

Romeo breaks down and bewails his fate in the Friar's cell, rejecting all the Friar's philosophical comforts; the Nurse finds him there and tells him to come to Juliet for their first night together.

Meanwhile old Capulet has decided to comfort Juliet for Tybalt's death by marrying her to Paris in two day's time.

Romeo and Juliet part at dawn, he to Mantua, she to learn from her mother of the plans for her wedding. She implores her parents to postpone the marriage, but her father is enraged, her mother will not listen, and the Nurse, thinking any husband better than none, advises her to forget Romeo and marry Paris.

Juliet goes to her last hope, the Friar.

Act III, scene i
Events now move so fast that the scenes seem to overlap. In the hot summer afternoon Mercutio is loafing around the streets looking for trouble (even today the homicide rate mounts with the temperature). Benvolio, as ever, tries to calm him, but in vain. Mercutio, pretending that he is describing Benvolio, in fact sketches a self-portrait, of a man 'as hot a jack in [his] mood as any in Italy' (12), who will quarrel for the slightest, or no, reason: 'Thou wilt quarrel with a man for cracking nuts, having no other reason but that thou hast hazel eyes:' (20). Benvolio, unwittingly forecasting Mercutio's death, says truly that such a man could not survive as much as an hour and a quarter.

Mercutio is accosted by Tybalt, also spoiling for a fight, and they exchange insults, while the agonised Benvolio in vain begs them to 'withdraw into some private place' (53). Romeo appears, and we know that he is returning from his wedding, full of happiness and goodwill to everyone, including the Capulets. We know also that he has not been home, so cannot have received Tybalt's challenge. Tybalt only knows that this young Montague dared to invade a Capulet gathering, and to gaze admiringly at young Juliet from behind his mask, so immediately Tybalt insults him: 'thou art a villain.' (63).

Normally this would be answered by an immediate challenge, so Mercutio is thunderstruck by Romeo's calm, polite answer to his new cousin-by-marriage: 'Villian I am none. Therefore farewell, I see thou knowest me not.' (67). Of course Tybalt has no idea what Romeo means, and this seems sheer cowardice. Tybalt is not to be thwarted. He mockingly calls Romeo 'boy', bidding him 'turn and draw'. Romeo still refuses to respond in kind to the insults and challenge, and Mercutio cannot bear his friend's 'calm, dishonourable, vile submission' (75). The 'gang' has been let down by its youngest member. Mercutio challenges Tybalt himself, and they set to.

Romeo desperately attempts to stop 'this outrage' (89) by reminding them of the Prince's commands. They pay no attention, so he rashly tries to come between them, which unsights Mercutio. Tybalt wounds Mercutio. and Tybalt and the Capulet suporters flee. Even when – as he is – fatally wounded, Mercutio jests, but bitterly. He has called Tybalt 'King of Cats', so his wound is a 'scratch', but nevertheless he declares that tomorrow he will be a 'grave man' – serious and no longer light-hearted, graved or cut up, and in fact in his grave. And indeed it is with deadly seriousness that he three times calls out 'A plague o' both your houses' (94, 103, 110) – a dying man's curse which will soon be fulfilled. Bubonic plague, with a mortality of some 70 per cent, was frequent in Shakespeare's London; there was a severe outbreak in 1593-4, just before this play was written.

Romeo has only been able to answer Mercutio's question, 'Why the devil came you between us?' (106) with the feeble, helpless response, 'I thought all for the best'. Now he realises that it is through his action (and lack of action) that Mercutio is dead, and that all his friends think him a coward, 'my reputation stained With Tybalt's slander' (115). Romeo rightly foresees that the consequences of this afternoon's work will lead to more disasters, but when the 'furious Tybalt' (125) comes back in triumph, 'rude will' triumphs over reason, and Romeo fights with him and kills him.

Romeo is stunned. 'O I am Fortune's fool' (140), he cries. Benvolio has to urge him to escape, while angry citizens throng the stage, and are joined (as the Folio instructs) by 'Prince, Montague, Capulet, their wives and all'. Lady Capulet wails for her nephew Tybalt, and calls on the Prince for revenge: 'For blood of ours shed blood of Montague' (153). Blinded by hate, she will not accept Benvolio's true account of the fray, and persists:

I beg for justice, which thou, Prince, must give.
Romeo slew Tybalt, Romeo must not live.   (184)

The prince recognises that Romeo, in killing Tybalt, was avenging the death of Mercutio, but he has had enough of the feud, and after promising to fine both houses very heavily, banishes Romeo from Verona, upon pain of death. '*Immediately* we do exile him hence,' he decrees; 'Let

Romeo hence *in haste*' (191, 197), thus emphasising the ever-increasing acceleration of events.

Act III, scene ii

Perhaps the most striking contrast between succeeding scenes now follows. The great stage has been crowded with gallants, citizens and finally all the surviving cast except Juliet. There have been murder and tumult, furious citizens and an angry Prince. The scene ends in hatred, rage and misery. But hardly is the stage cleared before Juliet, a small, solitary figure, absolutely unconscious of what has happened, radiant with joy and love, comes out on her balcony above and rapturously speaks her epithalamium, or wedding song, bidding night fall rapidly and swiftly bring Romeo to her loving arms (see page 73).

Juliet's ecstacy is broken in upon by the Nurse's hysterical entry, still carrying, with terrible irony, the rope ladder made to bring Romeo to his bride. Shaken by the murder, she can only cry 'He's dead, he's dead, he's dead' (37), so that Juliet thinks that it is Romeo who has perished. Juliet shows her confusion and despair by a long series of puns on 'I', 'Ay' and 'eye'.

> Hath Romeo slain himself? Say thou but 'Ay',
> And that bare vowel 'I' shall poison more
> Than the death-darting eye of cockatrice.
> I am not I if there be such an 'I';
> Or those eyes shut that make thee answer 'Ay'.
> If he be slain, say 'Ay';   (45)

and the Nurse chimes in: 'I saw the wound, I saw it with mine *eyes*. . .' (52). We must remember that to an Elizabethan puns were not feeble jokes found in Christmas crackers, but a serious literary device to enrich meaning. On the stage the speech (however tricky for the actress) conveys very well Juliet's confused and agitated state.

The Nurse then bemoans Tybalt, and Juliet is so bewildered that when at last the Nurse speaks clearly:

> Tybalt is gone and Romeo banishèd.
> Romeo that killed him, he is banishèd,   (69)

(banishèd is a key-word repeated often in this scene and the next), poor Juliet can only believe that she has been totally deceived in Romeo, and falls back on a well-known 'emblem': O serpent heart, hid with a flow'ring face! (73). The popular 'emblem books' contained drawings with symbolic meanings, sometimes with explanatory verses. In this case a plant, either flowering or laden with strawberries, was pictured with a hidden serpent twined round the stem, and Shakespeare uses it again in *Macbeth*: 'look like th'innocent flower, but be the serpent under 't' (I.v.67).

But when the Nurse joins in abuse, 'Shame come to Romeo!' (89), Juliet reacts strongly: 'Blistered be thy tongue For such a wish. . .O what a beast was I to chide at him!' (90). The Nurse is shocked: 'Will you speak well of him that killed your cousin?' (96). And Juliet suddenly knows which side she is on: 'Shall I speak ill of him that is my husband?' (97). She begins to realise the true state of affairs:

> Tybalt is dead, and Romeo banished. . .   (112)
> There is no end, no limit, measure, bound
> In that word's death; no words can that woe sound.   (125)

The sight of the rope ladder reminds her bitterly of her hopes and expectations, now destroyed. She is being widowed before she is a wife: 'I'll to my wedding-bed And death, not Romeo, take my maidenhead.' But the volatile Nurse, now pitying her nursling, and always ready to tuck a couple into bed, offers to go to find Romeo at Friar Lawrence's cell, and bid him come.

Act III, scene iii

It is in the Friar's cell that we now see Romeo, full of 'affliction' and 'wedded to calamity'. Lawrence tries to reason with him, pointing out how much better banishment is than death, but Romeo, as ever embodying passion and impulse, greets the Friar's well-meant, if ineffective, comfort with scorn. Romeo rants in a formal, elaborate way. Undoubtedly a modern reader finds it hard to take seriously his complaint that 'carrion flies' may light on Juliet's hand, while he is banished: 'Flies may do this but I from this must fly' (41). In performance this speech is often cut down, but it does convey the unbalanced depths of despair into which Romeo has plunged; his wild talk of poison and knives shows how easily in disaster he falls to extremes. The Friar attempts to console him with 'philosophy' and 'reason', but Romeo is deaf to argument, and flings himself to the ground in despair.

A sudden knocking at the door alarms the Friar, but it is only the Nurse, who is disgusted with Romeo's 'blubbering and weeping' (87) and calls on him 'for Juliet's sake, for her sake rise and stand' (89). Romeo does rise, but only to attempt to stab himself; the Nurse snatches the dagger from him as one would take a dangerous toy from a wayward child, and the Friar embarks on a long and formal sermon.

Romeo in this state, he says, has only the *form* of a man; his tears better suit a woman, and his literally un-reasonable behaviour (showing passion without the restraint of God-given reason) is that of a beast.

Suicide is a mortal sin leading to everlasting damnation (should we remember this at the end of the play?) and it will kill Juliet too if Romeo commits suicide. Unwittingly the Friar is prefiguring what actually happens.

You have 'shape, love and wit', the Friar goes on – a handsome appearance, the power to love, and keen intelligence – but now you are belying your manly appearance, and abandoning your love Juliet, while your distorted intelligence, instead of improving your life, is ruining it. You are like a soldier who has a flask of gunpowder with which to protect himself, but if he is careless and incompetent, he can instead blow himself up with it.

The Friar argues, in what may seem an infuriatingly complacent way, that Romeo has much to be happy about. Juliet is alive. Romeo was not killed by Tybalt. The Prince did not condemn Romeo to death, but merely to exile. These things are true, but it seems absurd for the Friar to say to the miserable and distraught Romeo 'Happiness courts thee in her best array' (141). But he does advise Romeo to go to comfort Juliet, and then to leave at dawn for Mantua. With a burst of unfounded cheerfulness Lawrence plans to 'blaze [announce] your marriage, reconcile your friends, Beg pardon of the Prince' (150) and joyfully welcome Romeo back.

Brooke describes his Friar:

> Not as the most was he, a gross unlearned fool,
> But Doctor of Divinity proceeded he in school.

Again Shakespeare takes the hint, and his Friar's sermon is composed according to the rules of rhetoric. The Elizabethan audience, who were accustomed to stand literally for hours listening to noted preachers, may have appreciated it as an extra pleasure tucked into the play. But to a modern audience it is apt to seem too lengthy and platitudinous, holding up the action, and the Nurse's admiring response,

> O Lord, I could have stayed here all the night
> To hear good counsel. O what learning is! (158)

often excites ironical laughter.

The Friar's discourse has at least given Romeo time to pull himself together; the Nurse goes off to warn Juliet of Romeo's coming, and after the Friar has promised to keep in touch, Romeo hastens after her.

Act III, scene iv

In the Capulet mansion Old Capulet is explaining to Paris that there has not been an opportunity to sound Juliet, mourning for Tybalt, about his wooing. But, secure in the belief that his little daughter will do whatever he advises, Capulet arranges that Paris will marry Juliet immediately.

It is Monday; Thursday will be the wedding day. An Elizabethan father, especially in a wealthy family where property was concerned, expected and usually received absolute obedience from his daughter. In *A Midsummer Night's Dream* Theseus tells the rebellious Hermia, 'To you your father should be as a god' (I.i.47) and her father Egeus states unequivocally, 'As she is mine, I may dispose of her' (I.i.42). This attitude Capulet assumes without thought, as a matter of course.

Romeo and Juliet has been called a 'tragedy of unawareness', and this scene certainly bears out that description. The Capulet parents think that Juliet is mourning for Tybalt - they have no idea that she has done more than glimpse Romeo. Meanwhile Juliet is receiving Romeo to consummate their marriage, with no idea of the plans her father and Paris are forming.

Act III, scene v

Even as Capulet goes off to bed, Romeo and Juliet appear on the balcony. Their conversation is a kind of aubade, or 'dawn song', the song of secret lovers forced to part by the coming of day - typified by the troubador's refrain, 'Ah God, Ah God, that day should come so soon' (see page 76).

Warned by the Nurse of Lady Capulet's coming, Romeo climbs down from the balcony, and the lovers part for ever. Romeo at the last moment tries to be optimistic:

> . . . all these woes shall serve
> For sweet discourses in our times to come.   (53)

Juliet, however, as earlier in the orchard scene, has a premonition:

> O God, I have an ill-divining soul.
> Methinks I see thee, now thou art so low,
> As one dead in the bottom of a tomb.   (54)

It is so indeed that she will next see him.

In answer to Lady Capulet's call Juliet joins her mother on the main stage, wondering why she is summoned and unable to hide her grief, so that even Lady Capulet must notice, and, asking what is wrong, rebuke her daughter for 'evermore weeping for your cousin's death' (69), and advise a more moderate amount of grief.

They have an extraordinary conversation in which Juliet speaks in riddles, conveying very different meanings to her mother (who believes her 'feeling loss' is Tybalt) and to the audience, who have just seen her parting from Romeo. Lady Capulet is still exhibiting her hatred, and calling for vengeance, suggesting that Juliet's tears are not for Tybalt's death, but rather because his murderer Romeo is still alive. 'Would none but I might venge my cousin's death' (86) says poor Juliet - for then Romeo would have nothing to fear. But Lady Capulet responds 'We will have vengeance for it, fear thou not', and plans to send a poisoner to Mantua to kill Romeo. (Few in the audience will have time to wonder how on earth she knows that he has gone to Mantua!)

Now Juliet speaks her longing for Romeo and her grief for Tybalt, but in such a way that Lady Capulet thinks she is demanding Romeo's death.

> Indeed I never shall be satisfied
> With Romeo till I behold him – dead –
> Is my poor heart so for a kinsman vexed. . .
> . . .O how my heart abhors
> To hear him named – and cannot come to him –
> To wreak the love I bore my cousin
> Upon his body that hath slaughtered him.   (93)

Dr Samuel Johnson thought that 'Juliet's equivocations are rather too artful for a mind disturbed by the loss of a new lover'; Perhaps her wits are sharpened by her sense of desperation. But worse is to come.

Brushing aside grief and revenge, Lady Capulet now tells Juliet the 'joyful tidings' (104) that in three days time, on a 'day of joy', Paris will make her a 'joyful bride'. How ironic the repeated emphasis on 'joy'. Juliet, horrified and shocked, can do nothing but object, yet still speaking with double meaning:

> I pray you, tell my lord and father, madam,
> I will not marry yet, and when I do, I swear
> It shall be Romeo, whom you know I hate,
> Rather than Paris.   (120)

'Tell him so yourself,' returns her callous mother.

Capulet enters and is vexed to find Juliet in tears, 'evermore showering' (130). He feels and speaks as an absolute ruler, in legal terms:

> How now wife,
> Have you delivered to her our decree?   (137)

When Lady Capulet indicates, in a brutal phrase and a foreboding one, that Juliet is unwilling – 'I would the fool were married to her grave' – Capulet cannot believe his ears. 'Doth she not give us thanks? Is she not proud?' (142). The wretched Juliet tries to show that she is grateful for his endeavours on her behalf, though hating their outcome, but Capulet, in an expressive speech written with masterly rhythm, at last realises what she is saying, and puts his foot down. She is disobeying her lord. She is a traitor to the family. If she won't go willingly to St Peter's Church, he will 'drag thee on a hurdle thither' (155), as traitors to the state were dragged to their execution. Even Lady Capulet is appalled by this fierce attack – or is it to Juliet that she calls 'Fie, fie! what, are you mad?' (157). Capulet will not listen to his kneeling daughter, but storms so violently that the Nurse tries to intervene, and is in her turn snubbed and silenced.

To the Elizabethan audience the authority of ruler over subjects was paralleled by the authority of parents over children, each absolute, and each part of the 'great chain of being', on which decency and order depended. Parents would sympathise with Capulet's feelings. He has done the very best he can for his beloved only child, arranged a match (and at this level of society almost all marriages were arranged) with a high-born gentleman, rich, young, well-educated, an ideal husband. He has actually fixed the wedding day with the bridegroom. And now this wretched little girl rejects the splendid future he has conjured up for her, and will make him look a fool in the eyes of Paris. Finally he completely loses his temper, and after another speech whose rhythm admirably expresses his rage and frustration –

> An you be mine, I'll give you to my friend;
> An you be not, hang, beg, starve, die in the streets,
> For, by my soul, I'll ne'er acknowledge thee,
> Nor what is mine shall never do thee good.
> Trust to't; bethink you; I'll not be forsworn –   (192)

He strides out, a bitterly hurt and disappointed man. Juliet turns to her mother: 'O sweet my mother, cast me not away.' (199), and again uncannily forecasts her own fate:

> Delay this marriage for a month, a week,
> Or if you do not, make the bridal bed
> In that dim monument where Tybalt lies.   (200)

Shakespeare has prepared us for Lady Capulet's cold cruelty, nevertheless it is painful:

> Talk not to me, for I'll not speak a word.
> Do as thou wilt, for I have done with thee.   (203)

As a desperate last hope Juliet turns to her nurse, who has for fourteen years cared for her and consoled her: 'Comfort me, counsel me.' Juliet feels herself caught in an inescapable trap; 'heaven' is working against her. To her horror the Nurse delivers the 'comfort' we might expect. She is not quite as outrageously cynical as Brooke's Nurse:

> The pleasures past before she must account as gain,
> But if he [Romeus] do return, what then? for one she shall have twain.

But the Nurse has no idea of love as an exclusive individual relationship; one man, she thinks, is as good as another.

'I think it best you marry with the County' (216).

Paris, says the Nurse, is 'a lovely gentleman'. The only 'use' of husbands is to make wives pregnant – Romeo will not be available, so why not take Paris? Juliet is staggered. She recovers enough to say, 'Well, thou hast comforted me marvellous much' (229). The Nurse, deceived, trots away to tell Lady Capulet that Juliet, having displeased her father, is off to 'make confession and to be absolved'. And poor Juliet, abandoned by father, mother and nurse, turns to her very last hope, the Friar, her mind, like Romeo's, turning to suicide: 'If all else fail, myself have power to die.'

Act IV

Summary
Juliet arrives at the cell to find Paris asking the horrified Friar Lawrence to marry them on Thursday, in two days time. Paris leaves, confident that the arrangement has been made. Friary Lawrence proposes a desperate plan; Juliet must take a drug which will plunge her into a death-like sleep for forty-two hours; her family will, according to custom, lay her in her best robes in the Capulet tomb. The Friar will send for Romeo, to carry her off to Mantua as soon as she wakes. Juliet, though full of apprehension, goes home with the potion.

Capulet is bustling round overseeing preparations for the wedding, when Juliet returns from the Friar, and humbly apologises to him for her disobedience. The relieved and delighted Capulet determines to have the wedding a day earlier, on Wednesday.

Juliet manages to go to bed alone, and in spite of almost overwhelming fear, swallows the potion. Meanwhile preparations for the wedding proceed through the night. In the morning, music heralds the arrival of Paris, and the Nurse, going to waken Juliet, finds her apparently dead. The Friar rebukes her lamenting parents, since Juliet has been 'advanced', not as they hoped by marriage, but better, by going to heaven, and he urges them to take her body to the tomb.

Act IV, scene i
Friar Lawrence is having his own troubles; Paris is with him, making plans for his wedding. The Friar is horrified: 'On Thursday, sir? The time is very short' (1). But Paris is very willing to agree to Capulet's 'haste' (3) and thinks that it is 'in his wisdom' that he 'hastes our marriage' (11).

Juliet joins them, to be greeted by Paris as 'my lady and my wife'. With remarkable self-possession she exchanges small-talk with him, rather as she did with her mother earlier.

PARIS: Come you to make confession to this father?
JULIET: To answer that I should confess to you.
PARIS: Do not deny to him that you love me.
JULIET: I will confess to you that I love him.
PARIS: So will ye, I am sure, that you love me.
JULIET: If I do so, it will be of more price
            Being spoken behind your back, than to your face.   (22)

The dialogue in alternate single lines (known as stichomythia) gives an artificial air to these exchanges. How different the tone from the sonnet Juliet spoke with Romeo when they first met! (I.v.91, see pages 23 and 73).

As when evading Lady Capulet earlier, Juliet speaks with double meanings:

PARIS: Thy face is mine, and thou hast slandered it.
JULIET: It may be so, for it is not mine own.   (35)

Paris thinks that she is agreeing with him, but she, of course, means that her face, like every other part of her ('take all myself', II.ii.49) is now Romeo's.

By implying that she is there for her devotions, Juliet gets rid of Paris, and as soon as she is alone with the Friar, shows her true state of mind, 'past hope, past care, past help' (45). The Friar brings no comfort, but confesses that the news of the proposed wedding 'strains [him] past [his] wits' (47). Juliet, desperate but resolute, says that if he cannot help her to avoid the marriage, she is determined to kill herself. Seeing her both desperate and determined, the Friar hesitantly suggests a 'remedy'. Juliet is willing to do literally anything rather than marry Paris, and while trying to impress the Friar with her resoluion, she unwittingly forecasts what will happen to her:

> Or hide me nightly in a charnel house,
> O'er-covered quite with dead men's rattling bones,
> With reeky shanks and yellow chapless skulls;
> Or bid me go into a new-made grave,
> And hide me with a dead man in his shroud. . .   (81)

This vivid and horrific description perhaps owes something to the unusually large 'charnel house' at Stratford, a building in which were stored bones disinterred from the churchyard.

Friar Lawrence's 'remedy' is indeed alarming. Juliet must first pretend willingness to obey her father. The night before the wedding, she must take a drug prepared by the Friar – we have already met him gathering medicinal 'precious-juicèd flowers', to prepare us for his proposal. This potion will send her into a death-like sleep for forty-two hours, after which she will wake unharmed. Thinking her dead, her family will obey 'form', the usual custom of the community, and will lay her, dressed in her finest clothes, in the Capulet tomb. Meanwhile the Friar will summon Romeo, who will watch her waken and carry her off to Mantua. The audience is given no time to ponder the rashness and danger of this scheme, for Juliet snatches at any plan, however terrifying, which will postpone her wedding. She seizes the vial: 'Love give me strength, and strength shall help afford' (125).

Even Friar Lawrence has been caught up in the prevalent haste, for he promises to send 'a friar with speed' to Mantua, to inform Romeo of the plan.

Act IV, scene ii

Capulet has earlier told Paris that because of Tybalt's death the wedding must be quiet – 'No great ado – a friend or two. . .some half-dozen friends' (III.iv.23). Yet when it comes to the point, we see him dispatching lists of guests to be summoned and hiring 'twenty cunning cooks' to give his daughter a fitting wedding-feast. But he is still thinking of Juliet as a 'peevish self-willed harlotry' (a term of playful contempt – nothing to do with harlots or prostitutes – meaning rather 'a naughty, perverse girl'). He greets her on her return from the cell in words which depend less on their strict meaning than on the tone in which they are spoken: 'How now, my headstrong, where have you been gadding?' (16). Has his rage subsided as quickly as it arose, and his affection for his daughter reasserted itself? Does he speak more in sorrow than in anger, or is he still infuriated? The director or actor – or reader – must decide, preferably by saying the words aloud in different ways. In any case Juliet's humble submission and begging of pardon rejoices her father: 'I am glad on't; this is well. Stand up. This is as it should be.' (28). 'Form' is re-established; the daughter obeys her father. From Capulet's point of view all is well.

As so often, Shakespeare has incorporated his stage directions in the text. Juliet says she has been 'enjoined by holy Lawrence to fall prostrate', and her father's 'Stand up' shows that she has indeed knelt at his feet.

Juliet's overacting of submission makes Capulet determined to bring forward the wedding by twenty four hours, to Wednesday. He brushes aside his wife's objection, 'We shall be short in our provision' (38). This is yet another step towards disaster, another impulsive gesture which hurries on the catastrophe. But for the moment Capulet is delighted; 'My heart is wondrous light Since this same wayward girl is so reclaimed' (46).

It is painfully ironic that it is Juliet's pretence of submission which leads directly to catastrophe. And it is no less ironic to hear Capulet declare of 'this reverend holy friar' that 'All our whole city is much bound to him' (21).

Act IV, scene iii

Juliet, knowing that she will never wear the clothes and 'ornaments' (IV.ii.34) which she and the Nurse have chosen as wedding garments, quickly gets rid of both the Nurse and Lady Capulet. Since her father has brought forward the ceremony, she cannot wait, but must swallow the potion that very night.

The substance of her soliloquy (a speech spoken when alone, and used by Elizabethan playwrights to disclose the character's genuine thoughts and intentions) owes much to Brooke's poem. But the manner of writing transforms it. We can compare Brooke's convoluted sentence:

> What do I know (quoth she)
> If that this powder shall
> Sooner or later than it should
> Or els not work at all?

with Shakespeare's natural-sounding lines:

> What if this mixture do not work at all?
> Shall I be married then tomorrow morning?   (21)

Brooke writes that Juliet's 'imagining' was so strong

> That she surmised she saw
> Out of the hollow vault,
> (A grisly thing to look upon)
> The carcase of Tybalt.

Shakespeare's Juliet imagines

> ...bloody Tybalt yet but green in earth
> Lies festering in his shroud.   (42)

As Juliet holds the vial, one dread after another sweeps through her mind. What if the drug does not work at all? Will she be compelled to use her dagger as a last resort? And can she trust the Friar? Perhaps he has really given her a deadly poison, so that no one will discover his part in her marriage to Romeo. How long will she sleep? Juliet imagines the horror of waking too soon, alone, finding herself 'stifled in the vault', surrounded by the bones of her ancestors; she piles horror upon horror, smells, shrieks, terrifying herself even further. Suddenly she envisages Tybalt's ghost returning to seek out Romeo, and crying – 'Stay, Tybalt, stay!' (57) she toasts her husband: 'Romeo, I come! this do I drink to thee.' (58). She swallows the drug, and (the original stage direction tells us) 'she falls upon her bed within the curtains', pulling them together as she falls behind them.

There was some sort of recess behind the great stage, which could be curtained off (see page 63), or perhaps a curtained four-poster Elizabethan bed had been pushed on to the back of the stage.

Act IV, scene iv

All through the bustle of preparation for the wedding festivities, which is continuous throughout this scene, the audience is aware that behind the curtains lies the unconscious Juliet, drugged or perhaps dead. But again the other characters, unaware of the situation, feel assured that she is simply asleep, gathering strength for the 'day of joy' (III.v.109) ahead.

The Capulets and the Nurse come in and out preparing for the feast. Expensive spices, quinces, baked meats – 'spare not for cost' (6) cries hospitable Capulet. He refuses to go to bed, recalling other sleepless nights: 'I have watched ere now All night for lesser cause' (9). Lady Capulet at once rebukes him for his womanising past, threatening 'I will watch you from such watching now' (12). Capulet disregards her unpleasantness, chivvying the servingmen, making bad jokes about a 'loggerhead' fetching logs, evidently in high good humour – which emphasises the difference between the situation as he sees it, and as it really is.

Throughout the scene there is constant reminder of time passing: 'the second cock hath crowed...'tis three o'clock' (3); 'Make haste, make haste' (16); 'Good faith, 'tis day' (21). Then music is heard – Paris must be arriving. Capulet goes to greet him and sends the Nurse (whose name, Angelica, we have just learnt) to wake Juliet. The sense of urgency is accentuated by the thrice-repeated 'Hie, make haste, Make haste. . .Make haste I say' (26) which ends the scene.

Act IV, scene v

Still we are kept in suspense. The Nurse does not at once go to the bed, but stands, perhaps adjusting her own wedding garments, or pinning on a nosegay, while she calls to Juliet by a variety of names, reminding us of all the different relationships they have had – 'mistress', 'Juliet', 'lamb', 'lady', 'slug-a-bed', 'Madam', 'bride'. She gets no response, even when she makes a typical bawdy joke:

> Sleep for a week; for the next night I warrant
> The County Paris hath set up his rest
> That you shall sleep but little.   (5)

'Set up his rest' is a phrase from an Elizabethan card game, primero, meaning 'staked everything he has'.

But when at last the Nurse goes to the bed, her alarmed cries bring the Capulets hurrying to the bedside, to discover their only child apparently lifeless. Their exclamations of horror and grief appear stilted: in times of great shock and distress such simple exclamations may be all that can be said, though Capulet does have one gentle and imaginative couplet:

> Death lies on her like an untimely frost
> Upon the sweetest flower of all the field.   (28)

The Nurse's cries of grief, in particular, are extremely crude, reminiscent of Shakespeare's parody of grief when Bottom as Pyramus laments Thisbe in *A Midsummer Night's Dream*. Lady Capulet's sentiments, find expression as,

> But one, poor one, one poor and loving child,
> But one thing to rejoice and solace in,
> And cruel Death hath snatched it from my sight.   (46)

She did not seem to 'rejoice and solace in' Juliet while she was alive.

Friar Lawrence enters with apparent calm, but surely with great inward anxiety. What answer does he expect to his question, 'Come, is the bride ready to go to church?' (33). Capulet's answer unwittingly sums up the end of the play:

> Death is my son-in-law, Death is my heir,
> My daughter he hath wedded. I will die
> And leave him all; life, living, all is Death's.   (38)

Lady Capulet, the Nurse, Paris and Capulet all continue their outbursts of grief. The Friar, with some hypocrisy, rebukes them, resorting to the same sort of 'philosophy' (III.iii.55) with which he tried earlier to comfort Romeo. Juliet has been 'promoted' to heaven; they wished for her 'advancement'; what advancement could be better than that? They should not grieve. He urges them to convey her quickly to the church and tomb – does he wonder if she will wake too soon?

In the circumstances his exhortations fall oddly on our ears:

> The heavens do lour upon you for some ill;
> Move them no more by crossing their high will.   (94)

But this last situation has not been engineered by the heavens, but by the Friar himself.

The scene ends with a curious little interlude of rather feeble punning, when the musicians who had accompanied Paris, to play for the wedding, are dismissed by the Nurse's man, Peter. This part was played by Will Kemp, the leading comic actor of the period (see page 59), and presumably this was the last opportunity to give the audience a glimpse of their favourite comedian. The last act is no place for fooling, even to Elizabethans who were used, as Sir Philip Sidney reminds us, to a mingling of 'hornpipes and funerals' on their stage.

Perhaps Shakespeare was not concerned to make this scene deeply felt; true grief is reserved for the real deaths which are to follow.

Act V

Summary
Romeo, in Mantua, is dreaming happily of reunion with Juliet, when his man Balthasar brings terrible news from Verona. Juliet is dead; he saw her funeral. There is no message from the Friar. Romeo immediately decides to die with Juliet. He buys a deadly poison from a starving apothecary, and rides off to Verona.

Friar Lawrence discovers that Friar John, the messenger taking the letter explaining Juliet's pretended death to Romeo, has been prevented from leaving Verona. Since now Romeo can know nothing of the Friar's scheme, Friar Lawrence decides to fetch the waking Juliet from the tomb and hide her in his own cell.

Paris comes to the Capulet vault to mourn his lost bride. He is horrified to find Romeo breaking into the vault, and attempts to stop this sacrilege. Romeo urges Paris to leave him; Paris attempts to arrest Romeo. They fight, and Paris is slain. Romeo lays his body, as Paris has asked, in the monument, and turns to Juliet.

She is still so beautiful that he can hardly believe that she is dead. But he will not pause; he drinks the poison and dies just before Friar Lawrence stumbles in, too late, to discover not only Romeo but Paris too, lying dead beside Juliet.

Juliet wakes, and the panic-stricken friar tries in vain to persuade her to run off with him before the 'watch' (men appointed to keep public order) arrive. He 'dare no longer stay' (159), and escapes, but Juliet will not part from her dead husband, stabs herself, and dies.

For the third time the stage fills with citizens, the Prince, Montagues and Capulets. Sad explanations are given by Friar Lawrence, who has been brought back by the watch. The Prince blames himself for his earlier leniency; he too has suffered by losing 'a brace of kinsmen' (294), Mercutio and Paris. Montague and Capulet are reconciled, but at what cost.

Act V, scene i

Later in this act Romeo will talk of condemned men 'at the point of death' being 'merry, which their keepers call A light'ning before death' (V.iii.89), and at the beginning of this scene this is what happens to Romeo himself. Just before he hears the shattering and fatal news of Juliet's death, he enters in high spirits. Romeo thinks his 'dreams presage some joyful news at hand' (2) and is full of 'cheerful thoughts' (5). He has been dreaming that he lay dead, but was revived by Juliet's kisses; he will indeed lie dead in her tomb, and be kissed, but not alas revived. We may remember that this is his second prophetic dream; before he went to meet Juliet for the first time he had 'dreamt a dream' (I.iv.50), and though interrupted by

Mercutio, returned later to his doubts, misgiving 'some consequence yet hanging in the stars' (I.iv.106) and even foreseeing his own 'untimely death' (111).

Romeo's man Balthasar arrives from Verona with the news of Juliet's death. He saw her funeral. Romeo immediately decides to defy fate, and the Prince's sentence, and return to Verona. He is 'pale and wild' (28) and Balthasar begs him to pause, to have patience. Uselessly, for Romeo has made his impulsive decision, clearly and simply expressed: 'Well, Juliet, I will lie with thee tonight' (34). Chance speeds him on his way – he has already seen the shop of a starving apothecary, so poor that he would probably be willing to deal illegally in poison. Romeo offers the man a large sum in gold ducats if he will supply an instant poison, so potent

> . . . that the trunk may be discharged of breath,
> As violently as hasty powder fired
> Doth hurry from the fatal cannon's womb.   (63)

Friar Lawrence earlier compared the 'violent delights' of Romeo's sudden marriage with 'fire and powder Which, as they kiss, consume' (II.vi.10). Romeo now rushes to death with the same vehemence and haste as he rushed to love.

The apothecary is easily bribed; Romeo hails the drug as 'cordial, not poison' (85), and hurries off to Verona.

Act V, scene ii

Friar John, who should have carried the news of the drugging of Juliet to Romeo in Mantua, was found in a plague-stricken house, kept in quarantine in Verona, and has to tell Friar Lawrence that his message had miscarried. Friar Lawrence is horror-struck, but does not know how grave the situation really is; he has no idea that already Balthasar has told his master that Juliet is dead. The time of Juliet's wakening is near, but Friar Lawrence, true to his precepts, has no sense of urgency. He imagines that there will be time to send another letter to Romeo, and that meanwhile he can hide Juliet in his cell. Again the contrast between Romeo's passionate impulse and the slow (and ultimately fatal) deliberation of the Friar is emphasised.

Act V, scene iii

Paris enters, with his page, who is carrying flowers and a torch – the latter an indication that it is already night. The scene is set by allusions to 'yond yew trees' (3) (trees which were planted in churchyards), to the 'hollow ground' of 'the churchyard', to 'digging up of graves', and the atmosphere is established by the page's nervous confession that he is 'almost afraid to stand alone Here in the churchyard' (10).

We are outside the Capulet vault, within which Juliet is lying on her tomb, and dead Tybalt on his. Paris speaks a verse of mourning (see page 72) and strews his flowers on the ground, but is interrupted by the entrance of Romeo and Balthasar, laden with tools for breaking into the vault. Romeo has written a letter to his father, and orders Balthasar to deliver it next morning, but now to leave him, threatening violence should he return. Romeo's intents are, as he says, 'savage-wild'; he is completely irrational. Dismissing Balthasar, he turns to the tomb. The 'hungry churchyard' (36), swallowing bodies, is already 'gorged with the dearest morsel of the earth' (46), that is, with Juliet; soon, says Romeo, he will offer it more food, his own body.

Paris, utterly unaware of the true situation, sees only a Montague committing sacrilege by breaking into the Capulet vault, presumably to desecrate it. He sees also a man who was banished on pain of death, and determines to arrest him.

Romeo only wants to be left alone. He tries to persuade Paris to leave him: 'Good gentle youth, tempt not a desperate man' (59). The 'young Romeo' is now speaking as if he were the elder of the two, addressing Paris again as 'youth' and 'boy' (61, 70). Paris pays no attention; he is determined to arrest this doubly criminal intruder. They fight; Paris's page, terrified, hurries off to fetch the watch. Paris falls; he begs Romeo to lay him beside Juliet; Romeo discovers that he has killed 'Mercutio's kinsman, noble County Paris' (75). He half-remembers Balthasar telling him that Paris was to marry Juliet. Was it a dream? Or some mad imagining?

Romeo drags the body of Paris into the vault, to share Juliet's grave, but this is no dark grave:

> A grave? O no, a lantern, slaughtered youth;
> For here lies Juliet, and her beauty makes
> This vault a feasting presence full of light.   (84)

Again Juliet symbolises light, a lantern such as a man might hold in his hand to shine against the blackness of the enveloping night and the grave; and this leads Romeo to think of the other kind of 'lantern', the little turrets (originally built along the roof of a great hall to let out smoke from central fires) from which light streams out at night. Juliet's beauty makes the vault 'a feasting presence', a presence chamber where the Queen might receive ambassadors to a feast – and this also recalls the feast where first they met, only four days earlier, but now infinitely distant.

Romeo hangs over Juliet, adoring her. His long speech must have held the first spectators of the play in suspense (see page 72). We know what will happen, but they must have wondered if the Friar would arrive – he was on his way – or Juliet awake, at any moment. Surely when Romeo says that 'death's pale flag is not advancèd' (96) in her cheeks, he might realise that this because she was not, in fact, dead?

It is remarkable that as he goes – as he thinks – to join Juliet in death, he uses the same language and images as when he was about to see her for the first time. At I.iv.106 we find 'stars. . .bitterly. . .death. . .expire. . . term. . .closed. . .forfeit. . .steerage. . .course. . .sail'. And now at V.iii.111 we find 'stars. . .seal. . .dateless bargain. . .death. . .bitter. . .pilot. . .bark'. Also, when talking with Juliet in the orchard, Romeo used the same image:

> I am no pilot, yet wert thou as far
> As that vast shore washed with the farthest sea,
> I should adventure for such merchandise.   (II.ii.82)

But now the 'fearful passage of their death-marked love' (Prol. 9) is at an end, and Romeo must 'now all at once run on The dashing rocks [his] sea-sick weary bark' (118), to final shipwreck.

We saw Juliet toasting Romeo as she drank the potion. Now Romeo in his turn cries 'Here's to my love!' (119), kisses Juliet, and falls dead beside her, just as Friar Lawrence stumbles into the churchyard and learns from Balthasar that Romeo is already 'in the Capels' monument' (127). The Friar is terrified: 'O much I fear some ill unthrifty thing' (136), that is, some evil piece of bad luck. But he advances, sees blood and discarded swords, and so discovers both Romeo and Paris dead. He immediately blames fate, or luck: 'Ah what an unkind hour Is guilty of this lamentable chance!' (145). And at this moment Juliet wakes, perfectly conscious and composed. Her last thought before her sleep was of Romeo (IV.iii.58) and so is her first waking thought:

> O comfortable friar, where is my lord?
> I do remember well where I should be,
> And there I am. Where is my Romeo?   (148)

The Friar is now panic-stricken and has completely lost his head. He offers no explanation, but again blames fate:

> A greater power than we can contradict
> Hath thwarted our intents.   (153)

To Juliet, waking triumphantly after her ordeal to meet her husband, he abruptly says that husband 'there lies dead; And Paris too', and offers to 'dispose' of her 'among a sisterhood of holy nuns' (157). And when she will not come, he scuttles off in alarm.

Juliet has no attention for anyone but Romeo. She realises that he has poisoned himself, and wishes that he had left a drop for her; she kisses his lips, hoping that they retain some poison. We hear the watchmen returning with the page, and Juliet realises that she has only a moment. She draws Romeo's dagger:

> Yea, noise? Then I'll be brief. O happy dagger!
> This is thy sheath; there rest, and let me die.   (168)

'Rest' occurs in the First Quarto; in the Second Quarto the word is 'rust'. The director may choose whichever he prefers; the changing of a single letter changes completely the images and implications called up by the word. Juliet stabs herself; her forebodings are justified; grave and wedding-bed are one (I.v.135, III.v.200).

All these events have happened very quickly, and the play has accelerated towards this deadly climax. This is where certain nineteenth-century productions ended. But Shakespeare had more to say.

The bewildered watchmen find Paris and Romeo dead, and stranger still, Juliet though 'two days buried' is 'bleeding, warm and newly dead' (174). The Friar and Romeo's man are brought to the Prince, roused by the commotion; the Capulets hurry in, to be thunderstruck by the sight of Juliet newly stabbed. Montague too appears, but not his wife; she has died from grief about Romeo's exile. Montague now discovers that he has lost Romeo also.

Friar Lawrence is called upon to explain what has happened, and sets forth the whole miserable story, describing the catastrophe as 'the work of heaven', but adding that 'if aught in this Miscarried by my fault, let my old life Be sacrificed' (265). Balthasar and Paris's page add their witness, and Romeo's letter to his father completes the sad story. The Prince, faced for the third time with the deadly effects of the feud, rebukes (as Mercutio did) *both* houses:

> Where be these enemies? Capulet, Montague,
> See what a scourge is laid upon your hate,
> That heaven finds means to kill your joys with love.   (290)

Nor does the Prince try to escape his own responsibility. It is the first duty of the Prince to preserve order in the state; he shut his eyes to the feud, and in consequence lost 'a brace of kinsmen' (293), Mercutio and Paris.

Capulet and Montague are reconciled at last, and each promises to raise a golden statue to the other's child. But it is all too late. Benvolio does not appear (though in one version of the play we hear of his death too) and every one of the younger generation is dead, 'poor sacrifices of [their] enmity' (303).

> Capulet spoke truly when he declared:
> Death is my son-in-law, Death is my heir,
> My daughter he hath wedded. I will die
> And leave him all; life, living, all is Death's.   (III.v.38)

6 CHARACTERISATION

The Lovers

Romeo and Juliet, hero and heroine, are certainly the main characters in the play; their relationship is its central interest. It is surprising, then, that they are together for only about one-ninth of the play – some 330 lines. The brevity of their encounters emphasises the fact that they have no time to get to know each other quietly, but have to snatch what moments they can; the intensity of their exchanges has to compensate for their brevity.

The Greek philosopher Aristotle said that poetry showed things not as they are, or were, but as they might be; perhaps this is what Shakespeare is doing here. Young love, sometimes called 'calf love' by those who have forgotten it, or never experienced it, can be quite as poignant as any emotion felt in later life. Shakespeare's Romeo and Juliet perish before their love has had time to alter or fade, and they remain, like John Keats' lovers in his ode, *On a Grecian Urn*, 'for ever panting and for ever young'.

We must remember that on the Elizabethan stage Juliet would be played by a boy actor, and the audience in the public theatre would not accept scenes of sensual love-making between a man and a boy, or two boys, so we are never shown intimate love-making. Their first meeting is in public, and at their second meeting, in the orchard, the lovers are physically separated – Juliet is out of reach, on her balcony, and Romeo has to leave 'so unsatisfied' (II.ii.125). The lovers are only once seen alone again, at their parting, a moment of the deepest emotion, but not of sensual love. Finally Juliet wakes to find Romeo dead. Only through poetry can Shakespeare create their passionate relationship, not through visible embraces.

But there is no doubt that their love is physical as well as mental and spiritual. When Juliet is waiting for Romeo to come to her after their wedding, her longing for night and her husband is so explicit that in the nineteenth century the passage was sometimes cut, as too improper. (See page 73.) And when they part in the cruel dawn, it is clear that their marriage has been consummated.

Juliet

Shakespeare has made Juliet very young indeed, fourteen as opposed to
Brooke's heroine of sixteen. Legally boys of fourteen and girls of twelve
could make binding marriage contracts. And in many ways Juliet is indeed
childlike. When we first meet her she seems a quiet, obedient little girl,
ready to do whatever her mother suggests, willing to 'like' the man her
father has chosen, but only as far as her parents permit it.

Again, she has a childlike trust in her Nurse, using her as a messenger to
Romeo, relying on her to conceal the marriage and to bring Romeo to her
chamber at night. The depth of this trust can be measured by Juliet's
horror when it is betrayed. When Juliet is abandoned by both angry
parents, and, turning to the Nurse for comfort, is told to forget Romeo
and marry Paris, she cannot believe her ears. Her bewildered 'Speak'st thou
from thy heart?' (III.v.227) is answered almost casually by the Nurse:
'And from my soul too, Or else beshrew [curse] them both'. To which
Juliet bitterly adds, in all seriousness, 'Amen' [So be it!]. The Nurse
totally misunderstands the sincerity of Juliet's ill-wishing, and entirely
misses the irony and misery of 'Well, thou has comforted me marvellous
much.' Off goes the Nurse, unconscious of having given offence; she would
be bewildered and amazed to learn that Juliet now thinks of her as 'Ancient
damnation! O most wicked fiend!' (III.v.134)

But by this stage of the play Juliet has been forced into maturity by the
series of disasters which have occurred. She is showing the qualities of
determination and courage which enable her to hide her anguish, and chat
wittily and apparently calmly with Paris at the Friar's cell; to agree to the
Friar's dangerous plan; to appear to accept her father's commands; to
drink the potion; finally, to kill herself.

Juliet is quick-witted throughout, from her first appearance and her
pert snub to the garrulous Nurse: 'And stint thee too, I pray thee, Nurse,
say I' (I.iii.58). How skilfully she responds in kind to Romeo's formal
approach, so that they speak their sonnet in perfect accord (see page 23).
Juliet shows her quick-wittedness again when she discovers Romeo's
identity; she is startled into lamenting aloud:

> My only love sprung from my only hate!
> Too early seen unknown, and known too late!
> Prodigious birth of love it is to me,
> That I must love a loathed enemy. (I.v.139)

But when the Nurse overhears and questions her, Juliet manages to brush
off her curiosity. 'What's this, what's this?' asks the Nurse, and Juliet
replies, 'A rhyme I learned even now Of one I danced withal' (I.v.143).

When Juliet comes out on her balcony after the ball, she still has the
same concern. The only thing that she knows about Romeo is that he is a

Montague, and that seems an insuperable obstacle. Let him renounce his name, she muses, 'And for that name which is no part of thee, Take all myself' (II.ii.50). Romeo can contain himself in silence no longer, and responds, and Juliet's first thought is again of the feud: 'Art thou not Romeo, and a Montague?' (II.ii.60). All her questions are practical. How did he get there? How did he find the way? Romeo's answers are fantastical – 'With love's light wings did I o'er perch these walls' – but his tone is far different from that of his earlier elaborate effusions about Rosaline.

Love is to some a tantalising game, as played, for instance, by Cressida, who has the 'cunning to be strange':

> Yet hold I off. . .
> Then though my heart's content firm love doth bear
> Nothing of that shall from my eyes appear.
>
> *Troilus and Cressida* (I.ii.287)

Juliet completely reverses this attitude:

> But trust me gentleman, I'll prove more true
> Than those that have more cunning to be strange.   (II.ii.100)

Towards Romeo Juliet never exhibits 'cunning', she is transparently sincere. But while Romeo is rhapsodising, she is realising how much 'too rash, too ill-advised, too sudden' their avowals of love may be. Nevertheless she responds once again with total generosity and 'infinite' love.

Romeo is lost in a happy dream; the moment is enough for him. But Juliet looks ahead:

> If that thy bent of love be honourable,
> Thy purpose marriage, send me word tomorrow.   (II.ii.143)

And again, while Romeo is still comparing the 'silver-sweet sound' of 'lovers' tongues' to 'softest music', Juliet is asking 'What o'clock tomorrow Shall I send to thee?' No thought of any relationship but honourable marriage crosses her mind; she must give all or nothing.

> And all my fortunes at thy feet I'll lay
> And follow thee, my lord, throughout the world   (II.ii.147)

– or else 'leave me to my grief'.

Next morning, after begging, scolding, importuning, coaxing and finally demanding, Juliet persuades the Nurse to tell her Romeo's plan. At once, as impulsive in her own way as her lover is in his, Juliet hurries off to Friar Lawrence's cell to be married.

Though absolutely without cunning towards Romeo, Juliet can still exert some cunning towards others. Dr Johnson remarked rather disapprovingly that Juliet 'plays most of her pranks under the appearance of religion'.

Her family believe that she is going tot he Friar's cell to shrift, that is, for confession and absolution, when in fact she is off to be married. She later uses the same excuse when she must seek the Friar's advice on the threatened marriage to Paris, when she banishes Paris from the cell, and the Nurse from her bedchamber, by implying her need for privacy for prayers.

Juliet is forced by a series of crises to grow up rapidly, and we can see her gathering strength to face each one in turn. The pain of Romeo's banishment and departure for Mantua is immediately succeeded by the horror of her father's plans for another wedding. Old Capulet, enraged and startled by the rebellion of one who had been an obedient, as well as a beloved, only child, treats her with positive cruelty. Lady Capulet, coldest of women, abandons her and (as we saw) Juliet's last hope, the Nurse, advises her to betray her husband.

So beset, Juliet has no choice but to agree to the Friar's desperate scheme. She has neither family, nurse, nor husband to support her: 'My dismal scene I needs must act alone' (IV.iii.19). We hear her, with a child-like piling of horror upon horror, imagining everything that could go wrong, but finally, realising that this is the only way to join Romeo, she courageously swallows the potion.

Coming, as it were, full circle, Shakespeare has given the waking Juliet a 'light'ning before death', a moment of hope and joy just before disaster, in three lines of child-like simplicity and immense pathos:

> O comfortable friar, where is my lord?
> I do remember well where I should be,
> And there I am. Where is my Romeo? (V.iii.148)

She stirs, sees the Friar, and believes for a moment that all has gone well. Then she is deserted yet again, for the last time. The distracted friar makes a perfunctory attempt to get her to come with him, then runs away in terror. Juliet realises that Romeo is dead. She pulls out his dagger, and courageous to the last, stabs herself. Her last act, immediate, determined and successful, still truly expressive of her love for Romeo, typifies every step she has taken throughout the play.

Romeo

Brooke's hero Romeus is a young gallant who is endeavouring to seduce Rosaline. Shakespeare's Romeo is a virgin (III.ii.13), whose immaturity and isolation makes him feel completely helpless when tragedy strikes. He is a youngster who consciously affects the fashionable pose of 'melancholy lover', 'stabbed with a white wench's black eye', sighing and sobbing for a 'pale hard-hearted wench, that Rosaline', as Mercutio tells us (II.iv.4, 15). Romeo spouts love poetry, using the

> Taffeta phrases, silken terms precise,
> Three-piled hyperboles, spruce affectation,
> Figures pedantical,
>
> *Love's Labour's Lost* (V.ii.407)

which the lover Berowne abandons for 'russet yeas and honest kersey noes' when he experiences sincere emotion, and which Romeo too will abandon when he truly falls in love.

Benvolio tries in vain to mock Romeo out of his affectation, but as soon as Romeo meets Juliet, and finds that she responds to his approach, he completely forgets Rosaline. 'Her I love now,' he tells Friar Lawrence, 'doth grace for grace and love for love allow' (II.iv.85). The Prologue to Act II assures us that now, instead of languishing hopelessly, 'Romeo is beloved and loves again.'

From first to last Romeo worships Juliet's beauty. At the Capulet feast he exclaims: 'I ne'er saw true beauty till this night' (I.v.54), and in the tomb: 'Death...hath had no power yet upon thy beauty' (V.iii.92). But he approaches her reverently, as a pilgrim to a saint. And this love does not plunge him into woe or solitary wandering or 'artificial night'; he is in the highest spirits from his first sight of Juliet until the tragedy of Mercutio's death. Very young ('boy' to Tybalt, 'young Romeo' to the Nurse) all Romeo's emotions are exaggerated. He is sometimes completely euphoric, intoxicated by the excitement of being not only in love, but beloved:

> ...come what sorrow can,
> It cannot countervail the exchange of joy
> That one short minute gives me in her sight.   (II.vi.3)

Alternatively he is in the depths of despair, 'with his own tears made drunk', 'blubbering and weeping' on the cell floor (III.iii.83).

Romeo's outstanding characteristic is his impulsiveness. No sooner does he see Juliet than he declares his love, leaps the orchard wall, and marries her within twenty-four hours of their first meeting. He tries to evade responsibility for Tybalt's death by calling himself 'Fortune's fool' (III.i.139), but since he has consciously flung restraint to the winds, and called on 'fire-eyed fury' to be his guide, he is already behaving with 'the unreasonable fury of a beast' (III.iii.110). The same rush to action instead of explanation leads later to the death of Paris.

In the two great crises, his banishment and his hearing that Juliet is dead, Romeo behaves in the same hysterical and uncontrolled manner. In the first, he has the Friar and the Nurse to restrain him; in the second he is without advisers or friends.

Is the cause of the final catastrophe the accidental detention of Friar John, or is it Romeo's unthinking immediate haste to buy poison and his rash speeding back to Verona and disaster? Like Juliet, Romeo has to face his final crisis alone; he is exiled in Mantua, and he has already (before he had any need of it) noted a poor apothecary who would probably be willing to deal in forbidden drugs. When he defies the stars, is he rejecting a God-given destiny, and hastening to suicide and damnation, or is he renouncing this world of accident and change, and joining Juliet in a 'world-without-end' union? Tragic heroes are traditionally ruined by some flaw in their character. Is this a play about a tragic hero ruined by his impetuosity, or is it, as Harley Granville-Barker, actor, producer and scholar, suggests, not 'a tragedy of fated disaster, but of opportunity muddled away and marred by ill-luck'? Which plays the greater part in producing the catastrophe, Romeo's character, or sheer chance?

Capulet

At the time he wrote *Romeo and Juliet* we may believe that Shakespeare was well acquainted with the young gallants who thronged the playhouses, whom he draws so convincingly in Mercutio, Benvolio, Tybalt and Romeo himself. But he may not yet have encountered their fathers; Capulet does not behave like the head of a noble house, but more like the father of a well-off bourgeois family, perhaps a Stratford alderman, making jokes with the ladies about their corns (I.v.18) and with servants about cooks licking their fingers (IV.ii.3). He himself is willing to 'play the housewife' (IV.ii.43) and to go his own errands, be a 'cot-quean' (IV.iv.6) and order drier logs.

He is open-handed and hospitable, encouraging his guests even while repressing Tybalt, welcoming the uninvited masquers, 'this unlooked for sport comes well' (I.v.31), and offering them refreshment before they leave. He sends for 'twenty cunning cooks' for his daughter's wedding, saying 'spare not for cost' (IV.iv.6).

Capulet comes out to the first brawl in the street calling for a sword, to his wife's mockery, but he does accept the Prince's rebuke, and thinks that he and Montague are old enough now 'to keep the peace' (I.ii.3). When Tybalt wants to expel the Montague Romeo from the feast, Capulet forbids him. He has heard well of Romeo, and in any case won't have fighting under his roof. Tybalt persists and we see short-tempered Capulet flare into a rage, snubbing Tybalt heartily.

Capulet hesitates when even so eligible a suitor as Paris wishes to marry his only child and heiress, Juliet, because she is so young. But despite his proviso that Paris must 'woo her...get her heart' (I.ii.16), Capulet, like every Elizabethan father, is confident that Juliet will be 'ruled in all respects' (III.iv.13) by him. And when Lady Capulet first proposes the match to Juliet, her daughter meekly agrees.

In George Chapman's play *Eastward Ho* the goldsmith Touchstone tells his daughter Mildred that she is to marry his apprentice, and she replies: 'Sir, I am all yours; your body gave me life; your care and love, happiness of life. . .to your wisdom I wholly dispose myself.' Capulet must be expecting some such grateful response. Instead, Juliet refuses the young, handsome, rich and well-connected suitor he has provided for her.

Startled astonishment and disappointment make him extremely angry. He has been let down by his beloved daughter. It is a severe shock, and he shouts at her, threatens to wash his hands of her, and storms out.

When Juliet returns humbly from the Friar's cell, and submits, the overjoyed Capulet flings himself into preparations for the wedding. His horrified grief, when the bride is summoned in vain, is obviously genuine. And at the end, when, too late, he realises what their 'enmity' has done, he can even share Montague's grief.

Tybalt and Mercutio

Two young men barely mentioned in Brooke's poem are developed by Shakespeare into important characters, Tybalt and Mercutio. Tybalt in Brooke is simply a young man 'exercised in feats of arms', who 'with furious rage' led the Capilets against the Montagues. Shakespeare's Tybalt, full of 'wilful choler' (I.v.90), establishes in his first lines his fiery nature:

> Turn thee, Benvolio, look upon thy death. . .
> What, drawn and talk of peace? I hate the word.   (I.i.72)

Shakespeare uses him to display the state of warfare between the two families, and to spark off the first street fighting. So we are not surprised when Tybalt, offended by Romeo's intrusion at the Capulet feast, and by his obvious admiration of Juliet, calls for his rapier: 'To strike him dead I count it not a sin' (I.v.60). Since Capulet won't have fighting at his feast, the thwarted Tybalt can only retire, uttering threats.

He next meets Romeo in the street, and Tybalt seizes the opportunity to challenge him. But the newly-married, euphoric Romeo refuses to fight him, and Mercutio as well as Tybalt thinks Romeo a coward. When Mercutio fights in his place and is slain, Romeo forgets his new relationship, tries to avenge his friend, kills Tybalt, and is banished. From our first two glimpses of Tybalt, the later challenging and fighting seems natural, and the succeeding disasters inevitable. Shakespeare uses him to give emphasis and coherence to the plot.

In Brooke, Mercutio is simply a courteous courtier with very cold hands. At the Capulet feast he holds one of Juliet's hands in his chilly grip, while on the other she feels the burning heat of Romeo's fevered touch. Shakespeare made Mercutio high-spirited, volatile, witty, self-assured, sensual. It is such a dazzling part that some leading actors have preferred to play it rather than be Romeo. It has even been suggested that Mercutio had to be killed in Act III (when the victim might have been an Montague, say Benvolio) because he was distracting the audience's attention from the comparatively mild Romeo. In fact there could be no place for Mercutio's high spirits in the tragic second half of the play.

Mercutio is certainly a foil to Romeo. He is a sensual man who has no patience with any man's 'groaning for love' (II.iv.94), and he makes many blue jokes when teasing Romeo. An audience might find the orchard scene *too* sweet, too sentimental. But Mercutio's outrageous invocation of Rosaline, just before it, is so coarse and insensitive that the audience turn to the young lovers with relief and pleasure.

Mercutio rejoices when in II.iv Romeo appears to have shed his melancholy, and they vie in uttering ridiculous nonsensical puns. Mercutio believes that a man should be his true self, should take things as they come, and should take his place in society. 'Now art thou *sociable*, now art thou Romeo' (II.iv.95). To enjoy solitude could be the mark not only of a lover, but of a villain. 'I am myself alone,' says Shakespeare's blackest villain, the future Richard III, declaring his hatred of society, and 'I follow but myself,' says wicked Iago (*3 Henry VI*, V.vi.83; *Othello*, I.i.58).

Mercutio scorns affectation, whether of the melancholy lover or the fashionable 'duellist'. This word, new to an Elizabethan audience, he applies to Tybalt, a man who lives according to the latest fashion, a 'fantastico', a 'fashion-monger' (II.iv.31, 35), 'a braggart. . .that fights by the book of arithmetic' (III.i.105).

When Romeo is publicly insulted by Tybalt, and (against all the rules by which these gallants live) refuses to fight, Mercutio cannot bear this 'calm, dishonourable, vile submission' (III.i.75) and fights Tybalt himself.

Mercutio (like the Nurse) is one of the main sources of comedy in the first half of *Romeo and Juliet*. But each of them has one deadly serious moment, the Nurse when Juliet utterly rejects her advice (III.v.213-33) and Mercutio when he is wounded (III.i.95-112). Shakespeare uses the fatally wounded Mercutio as a Chorus, to point out the moral of the play, the idiocy of the feud. This splendidly vital young man is killed – and for nothing. His thrice-repeated dying curse (echoing the citizens' cries in Act I), 'A plague o' *both* your houses!' will be realised by the end of the play.

The Nurse

The play contains comedy as well as tragedy. Bottom in *A Midsummer Night's Dream* and the Nurse in *Romeo and Juliet* – each of them hearty, unselfconscious and egotistical – are the first of Shakespeare's major comic figures who are fully integrated and essential to the play. The Nurse has usually been played as an old lady (Ellen Terry was 71, Beatrix Lehmann even older), but only eleven years earlier the Nurse had been wet-nurse to Juliet, a post only given to the young and healthy. This would place her in her early thirties at latest.

She is full-blooded, gross but good-natured and, it seems, truly fond of Juliet. In fact it seems at first that the Nurse has taken the place of the cold Lady Capulet, as surrogate mother. Shakespeare has given her very free blank verse (printed in one Quarto as prose) and her speech when we first meet her in I.iii is colloquial, repetitive, full of oaths, interjections and irrelevancies, and spiced with bawdy jokes.

Taken into Juliet's confidence, she acts as messenger to Romeo, and refuses to be put down by Mercutio's impudence. She only has the briefest moment of prudence, when she warns Romeo not to lead Juliet 'into a fool's paradise. . .for the gentlewoman is young' (II.iv.173). But when she returns, to tell Juliet to go to the Friar's cell to be married, the Nurse delights in teasing her. She is 'aweary', her 'bones ache', she is 'out of breath', she has a headache and a backache, and as Juliet gets more and more impatient the Nurse deliberately tantalises her, going far beyond affectionate teasing and showing complete insensitivity.

Again, when the Nurse has to bring the terrible news of Tybalt's death, she makes no effort to soften the blow nor to help Juliet, in her distress, to bear it. When Juliet is cast off by both parents the Nurse, not positively evil, but simply unconcerned by questions of morality, and completely without conscience, shows how little she understands her nursling, and also how lightly she holds the marriage vow, by advocating bigamy. She has no idea of Juliet's loyalty, depth of feeling, resolution and courage.

Dr Johnson has summed her up: 'The Nurse is one of the characters in which the Author delighted; he has, with great subtilty of distinction, drawn her at once loquacious and secret, obsequious and insolent, trusty and dishonest.' The actress playing the part must decide which of these contradictory qualities she intends to emphasise.

Here, as so often in Shakespeare's plays, the text can be interpreted in several ways; the director, actor or reader must undertake the task of interpretation.

Friar Lawrence

Romeo and Juliet is a symmetrical play. Two families, 'both alike in dignity', each have an only child, and each child has an elderly adviser and friend, who in the end is a broken reed. Like the Nurse, Friar Lawrence at first appears to be helpful and sympathetic, even wise, certainly well-meaning. But despite his moralising, 'Wisely and slow, they stumble that run fast' (II.iii.94), and 'Too swift arrives as tardy as too slow' (II.vi.15), he makes no attempt to persuade Romeo to delay, or to tell his parents his wishes. The Friar rashly marries the lovers as soon as Romeo asks him.

Lawrence shelters the banished Romeo in his cell, but all he can do is to philosophise, and it is the Nurse who makes the 'blubbering and weeping' Romeo 'stand up...rise and stand' (III.iii.88) and snatches the dagger from him.

Despite the Friar's expressed hope that the marriage may 'turn your household's rancour to pure love' (II.iv.92) he does nothing whatever to bring this about. When it seems that his involvement in the marriage may be discovered, the Friar, strained 'past the compass of [his] wits' (IV.i.47), never thinks of confessing to the Capulets or Montagues, and thus endeavouring to reconcile them, but involves Juliet in what is indeed a 'desperate' scheme, a very dangerous plot that the least accident could ruin.

Easily thrown into panic – for instance when the Nurse knocks on the cell door when Romeo is concealed within – Lawrence cannot cope with the final horrors. Arriving too late to save Romeo, he deserts Juliet: 'I dare no longer stay' (V.iii.139). Is it with scorn or pity that Juliet responds, 'Go get thee hence, for I will not away'? The Friar shifts the blame to some 'greater power' (V.iii.153), 'accident' (250), 'this work of heaven' (260) and does not seem to think that the scheme miscarried through any fault of his.

Did it? Nancy Mitford's 'Uncle Matthew', in *The Pursuit of Love*, was taken to *Romeo and Juliet*. 'He cried copiously, and went into a furious rage because it ended badly. "All the fault of that damned padre," he kept saying. . .still wiping his eyes, 'That fella, what's 'is name, Romeo, might have known a blasted papist would mess up the whole thing."'

Comedy: Peter

In Elizabethan 'mixed' plays comedy was added to tragedy by inserting totally irrelevant crude interludes, often inspired by a mischief-maker, the 'Vice'. In Thomas Preston's tragedy *Cambyses* three ruffians, Huf, Ruf and Snuf, fight over a whore and are beaten by her; later the Vice sets on Hob and Lob to fight each other; Hob's wife parts them and attacks the Vice with her broom, 'she gets him down and he her down – one on top of another makes pastime', with such jests as 'Oh, oh my heart, my heart! O my bum will break!' The Vice also joked directly with the audience, and this power of impromptu funning was the hallmark of the great comic actor Richard Tarlton, and his successor Will Kemp.

When the Earl of Leicester went fighting in the Low Countries, he took with him his company of actors; Sir Philip Sidney wrote in 1586 about this same Will Kemp, 'my Lord of Leicester's jesting player'. Leicester died in 1588 and the company dispersed, Kemp joining Lord Strange's Men (which became Shakespeare's company) and becoming famous for his 'extemporal wit'. We know that Will Kemp played Peter in *Romeo and Juliet*, which seems an astonishingly minor part for a leading actor (and sharer) in the company.

Peter has no necessary function in the play. When he enters escorting the Nurse in II.iv he has but one word in the text: 'Anon' – that is, 'Coming'. This could imply that he is fooling around instead of attending on her, or perhaps he is imitating her manner with her fan. His second speech is a bawdy retort to the Nurse's complaint that he is standing by and allowing 'every knave to use me at his pleasure' (IV.ii.162), and his third and last is again the single word 'Anon'. Surely he must have been showing his 'extemporal wit' and delaying, so that she orders him 'before and apace'. In the next scene he enters only to be sent away (II.v.20) – a complete waste of actor and time unless there was more fooling – and finally, after Juliet's supposed death, Peter enters to the musicians (IV.v.100). The feeble punning that follows can only have amused the audience because *anything* done on the stage by Will Kemp seemed funny.

We can imagine how unwillingly Shakespeare allowed Kemp's impromptus when we read in *Hamlet* (after Kemp had left the company):

> Let those that play your clowns speak no more than is set down for them; for there be of them that will themselves laugh, to set on some quantity of barren spectators to laugh too, though in the mean time some necessary question of the play be then to be considered, that's villainous.   (III.ii.37)

But in 1595 Kemp was a very important member of the company, and we can imagine him stretching his short 33 lines regardless of the author, and winning the laughter of the 'barren spectators'.

7 THE PLAY ON THE STAGE

7.1 STAGE HISTORY

It is thought that *Romeo and Juliet* has been produced more often than any other of Shakespeare's plays except *Hamlet*. The title pages of the first three printed versions, in 1597, 1599 and 1609, speak of many perform-ances. There are several contemporary mentions of its popularity. John Marston in 1598 asked a stage-struck gallant 'What's played today?'

> I set thy lips abroach, from whence did flow
> Naught but pure Juliet and Romeo.

'Sweet Mr Shakespeare' was mentioned in an undergraduate play at Cambridge, in which one character wooed his lady with 'monstrous theft' from *Romeo and Juliet*. 'Romea' was spoken of in 1599 as a splendid creation of 'honey-tongued Shakespeare'. In 1623, in the First Folio Leonard Digges wrote that it was impossible

> with some new strains t'out-do
> Passions of Juliet, and her Romeo.

And sure enough, constant productions have proved him right.

The theatres were closed by the Puritans in 1642, but reopened with Restoration of King Charles II in 1660; within two years Betterton, the leading actor of the period, was playing Mercutio. Before 1665 a curious version of the play appeared, a tragi-comedy, which on alternate nights ended happily, 'preserving Romeo and Juliet alive', and adding a mysterious character called 'Count Paris's wife'.

In 1680 Otway wrote a play about the feud of Marius and 'Sylla' in Republican Rome, and inserted the love story from *Romeo and Juliet*, calling the lovers Young Marius and Lavinia; this was played for some sixty years. In 1744 Theophilus Cibber concocted something more like Shakespeare's original, and played Romeo opposite his sister as Juliet. This however was soon superseded by Garrick's *Romeo and Juliet* at Drury Lane, altered by the abolition of Rosaline, by making Mercutio deliver the Queen Mab speech at dawn in 'a wood near Verona', and by making Juliet waken just after Romeo had drunk the poison, too late to save him, but in time to have a long and affecting farewell scene. This version was acted till 1845. Garrick's other innovation, a grand funeral procession for Juliet, with dirges, 'in the inside of a church', was included in most productions until 1878.

From 1750 until 1800 there was only one year when the play was not staged; and indeed in 1750 there were twelve days in which no other play was on in London, since the only two licensed theatres, Covent Garden and Drury Lane, were both staging *Romeo and Juliet* with rival casts. The story goes that when Juliet cried to Garrick, 'Romeo, Romeo, wherefore art *thou* Romeo?' a man in the gallery shouted, 'Because Barry's gone to Covent Garden'. From 1761 Garrick gave up the part of Romeo (he was aged forty-four) but still scored a great success as Mercutio.

The stage history of the play in the nineteenth and twentieth centuries includes all the great names of the English stage, but it was two American sisters, Charlotte and Susan Cushman, playing Romeo and Juliet respectively, who restored all of Shakespeare's text in 1845, killing Garrick's version. No fewer than fourteen actresses have played Romeo: is there any other of Shakespeare's heroes who could plausibly be played by a woman?

The most memorable twentieth-century production was perhaps that of 1935, in which John Gielgud and Laurence Olivier played alternately Romeo and Mercutio, with Dame Peggy Ashcroft as Juliet and Edith Evans as the Nurse.

In the second half of the nineteenth century stage scenery and settings grew more and more elaborate, and these took so much time to set up and take down that the text of Shakespeare had to be very heavily cut. In 1882 Sir Henry Irving was Romeo in a highly-praised production, which had thirteen distinct pictorial scenes – 'a marvel of scenic success', said a critic. The balcony, for instance, was 'solidly built up with marble pillars, shaded in front by quivering foliage'; Juliet's chamber was amply furnished; there was a much-admired 'secret place in the monastery', and finally two distinct sets for Act V, scene iii.

The Juliet, Ellen Terry (who was to play the Nurse in 1919), described how at rehearsal Irving 'kept on saying "I must go *down* into the vault". . . He had the exterior of the vault in one scene, the entrance to it down a flight of steps. Then the scene was changed to the interior of the vault, and the steps now led from a height above the stage. At the close of the scene when the Friar and the crowd came rushing down into the tomb, these steps were thronged with people, each one holding a torch, and the effect was magnificent.' Doubtless it was magnificent, but was it Shakespearean?

Surely the last scene must move swiftly without any interruption from the entrance of Paris to the end of the play.

It is obvious that Irving's production, requiring so many and such elaborate scene changes, must have been broken up into a series of short scenes, with considerable pauses between them. And this is almost certainly the antithesis of the continuous, swiftly-moving performance given originally by Shakespeare's own company at the Globe.

7.2 SHAKESPEARE'S THEATRE

We do not have a complete description of any one of the many Elizabethan public theatres, though there exists a sketch of the Swan Theatre about 1596, by a visitor from abroad, and a builder's contract for the Fortune Theatre, built by the Admiral's company to rival Shakespeare's Globe. But it is generally agreed that the outer shape was roughly circular, open to the sky, and that there was a very large stage which stuck out into the yard (see page 83).

Two great posts (which could be used as columns of a palace, or trees in a forest, or masts of a ship) held up the 'heavens' or 'shadow', a roof which protected the rear of the stage. In this there was a trapdoor through which thrones or clouds or comets could be let down, and firecrackers slid down cords to represent lightning.

The stage itself had trapdoors, through which magic trees, devils and apparitions could rise, or characters descend to caves, cellars and, as in medieval mystery plays, to hell.

At the back there was some sort of recess, which could be curtained off and hidden, or disclosed, and where 'discoveries' could be made. Juliet at the end of IV.iii 'falls upon her bed within the curtains', and is discovered there by the Nurse at the beginning of IV.v.

There was some sort of large entrance door at each side, and a balcony or gallery above – essential for _Romeo and Juliet_, as a balcony outside Juliet's room, but used in other plays as castle battlements, city walls, or just the upper part of a house.

There was no way of concealing the great stage; dead bodies had to be carried off in full sight of the audience.

There is no record of 'scenery' in the modern sense of painted flats, but a glance at the pictures of the elaborate triumphal arches designed and manned by actors for King James I's coronation procession in 1604, or the Elizabethan hall of an Oxford or Cambridge college, suggests that the permanent stage would be richly decorated. The poet Edmund Spenser and his friend Gabriel Harvey each described the stage as 'painted', and the pillars on the Swan stage were 'painted in skilful imitation of marble'.

It cost a penny to stand in the yard round the great stage, and twopence to sit on a bench in the galleries surrounding it above. The audience were noisy and obstreperous, and mewed like cats if displeased. The playwright had to catch their attention at once, and keep it throughout.

7.3 SHAKESPEARE'S STAGECRAFT

In the First Folio *Romeo and Juliet* is headed 'Actus Primus. Scaena Prima' – Act I, scene i. But there are no other divisions at all; the action is continuous from beginning to end. Later editors divided the text into acts and scenes – very oddly, in some cases, as II.i ends with the first line of a rhyming couplet, completed by the first line of the next scene. The extreme contrast between Mercutio's grossest bawdiness and Romeo's innocent passion can only be appreciated if they are experienced without a break between.

Romeo and Juliet is a fairly early play, but Shakespeare's stagecraft is already masterly. He does not begin with a classical exposition of what has been happening, but (after the Chorus's brief sonnet) shows us the feud in action. Four servants exchange words, then blows; others join in; every available actor is engaged; the stage is covered with struggling figures. The entry of the enraged Prince quietens the tumult, and he satisfies the audience's curiosity about the cause of the riot.

The play proceeds with a series of contrasts, from the crowd scene of riot and reproof to Benvolio's lyric poetry about dawn, and the introduction of the solitary 'melancholy' Romeo with his affected verses. Other striking examples are at the end of II.i (already mentioned), at the end of II.vi when the ecstatic lovers going to their wedding are followed in III.i by Mercutio hotly looking for a fight; above all, at the end of III.i when, after the disturbance and horror of hate, murders and banishment, Juliet comes out on her balcony alone, unaware and overflowing with love.

7.4 DRAMATIC IRONY

In Shakespeare's comedies he makes much use of dramatic irony, which is sometimes called 'discrepant awareness'; that is, a situation in which the audience, and sometimes certain characters, are aware of facts not known to others on the stage. The ensuing talk at cross purposes can lead not only to comic but also to tragic results, clearly seen in *Romeo and Juliet*.

When Romeo falls in love with Juliet, he thinks the only obstacle is the feud. But we know, as he does not, that Capulet has already accepted Paris as Juliet's husband, and that this will eventually cause tragedy. The catastrophe in III.i is largely due to lack of knowledge. Romeo (and the audience) do know that he is married to Juliet, and therefore he is now Tybalt's kinsman. Tybalt knows that Romeo admires Juliet, but has no idea that they have done more than speak at the feast. Mercutio and Benvolio never dream that Romeo is not still mooning after Rosaline; they (and the audience) learnt in II.iv that Tybalt has already sent a challenge to Romeo at his father's house. The audience alone know that Romeo has not been home to find it, and is therefore quite unprepared for Tybalt's attack. The audience understands Romeo's riddling speech to Tybalt about 'the reason that I have to love thee' (III.i.64) but to the other young men it appears rank cowardice.

Again and again, as when Juliet talks to her mother in III.v and to Paris in IV.i, speakers are at cross purposes. And since a little quiet thought and talk might clarify these situations, Shakespeare hurries on the characters before they can pause and clear up the misunderstandings.

Hence many scenes almost overlap in time. At the very moment that Romeo and Juliet are being married, Mercutio is refusing to retire peaceably, and he and Tybalt are already quarrelling when the newly-married Romeo meets them. Again, the banished Romeo is running to hide in the Friar's cell while Juliet is rapturously waiting to embrace him. The Nurse starts out to fetch Romeo to Juliet when he is already 'weeping and blubbering' in the cell. How ironic that as the marriage is being consummated, Capulet is promising Juliet to Paris, and as he sends his wife to prepare Juliet for the new wedding, Romeo and Juliet appear together on the balcony above. Any curtain-dropping and scene-changing would completely ruin the suspense of the audience: will Lady Capulet find Romeo with her daughter?

It is this speed, surely, this refusal to wait a moment, on the part of Capulet as well as of Romeo, that finally helps to cause the tragedy.

7.5 ESTABLISHING PLACE

The theatrical illusion on Shakespeare's stage comes from the characters, their speech and actions; when he wants them to be in a particular place at a particular time, Shakespeare makes this clear; when it does not matter, no time is wasted in unnecessary descriptive detail.

In *Romeo and Juliet* there is no need for painted backcloths. The Chorus has told us that we are in Verona, and Sampson and Gregory are clearly in some public place, a street or a square. In I.ii Capulet and Paris may plausibly appear in the same place, as Capulet returns from his interview with the Prince, and later Benvolio and Romeo come through it to meet Capulet's servant.

In I.iii we meet Juliet, her mother and her nurse – clearly at home, which can easily be conveyed by Lady Capulet sitting on a stool with a piece of embroidery in hand. At the end of the scene a servant summons them in through the curtains to the feast within, establishing this as the Capulet mansion.

The original stage direction then goes: *'Enter Romeo, Mercutio, Benvolio with five or six masquers: torchbearers.'* 'Torchbearers' – so evening has come; and 'masquers' – so they are in some sort of fancy dress, perhaps dressed as pilgrims, which would fit in very well with Romeo's approach to Juliet. They must carry masks, because later Mercutio puts his mask on – 'Give me a case to put my visage in' (I.iv.29) – and speaks of its 'beetle brows'. At the feast we know that Romeo too must be masked, for he is 'covered with an antic face' (I.v.57) and Tybalt only recognises him 'by his voice'. In a small town like Verona they must have often seen each other, and Tybalt recognises the unmasked Romeo at once (and fatally) in III.i. The masquers discuss the best way to enter, and when they are ready Romeo cries 'On lusty gentlemen' and Benvolio orders 'Strike drum' (I.iv.113).

The original stage directions are explicit: *'They march about the stage and servingmen come forth with napkins.'* The young men march round the perimeter of the great stage, while servingmen come through the curtains chattering and clearing away remains of the feast within. As the marchers reach the back of the stage, *'Enter all the guests and gentlewomen to the masquers.'* They have finished their feast and come out to see what is going on. Capulet, reminded of his own masquing days, welcomes the gatecrashers, and urges his guests to dance, the musicians to play, the servants to bring more lights. It is obvious that the stage is now Capulet's great hall.

Romeo (as he planned) has not joined the dance. As he looked on he has seen Juliet, and everything has changed. He watches to see where she will be when the dance ends, and determines to touch her hand. But Tybalt has heard Romeo's voice, and while the music and dancing continue in the centre rear of the stage, Capulet and Tybalt argue at one side, then Romeo waylays Juliet at the other, and they speak their sonnet (see pages 23 and 73). To give them privacy, the masquers may be performing some dance at the back of the stage, with the guests crowding round to watch, their backs to Romeo and Juliet. Masquers were expected to put on some slight show, dancing or fencing or singing.

At the end of the scene the young men retire through the side doors, the Capulets retire into their house through the curtains, and (after a second Chorus) Romeo returns, unable to tear himself away from the house where Juliet lives. Benvolio and Mercutio come back to look for him, in vain, for he hides, and when they go off home Romeo is overwhelmed to see Juliet appear above – obviously on a balcony outside her room, since we saw her retire below. We will see her there twice more, once blissfully longing for Romeo on her wedding day, and once miserably saying her last farewell to him as he goes off to Mantua and banishment.

Similarly right through the play no programme notes about place are needed; all is in the text. And Shakespeare frequently makes a character at the end of a scene say where he or she is going, so that we will know where we are when next we see them. For instance, Romeo leaves for 'my ghostly father's cell' at II.ii.188, the Nurse tells Juliet to be off to the Friar's cell at II.v.69; Juliet in desperation determines to go 'to the friar to know his remedy' at III.v.240, and in each case this is where they shortly appear.

7.6 ESTABLISHING TIME

The modern producer has immense technical resources; he can have any degree of lighting from a fiery glare to a murky darkness; moonlight is no problem. Shakespeare however had nothing but words, and he had to convince an audience in broad daylight that they were seeing two lovers meeting by moonlight.

Quince and his amateur actors in *A Midsummer Night's Dream* appreciated the difficulty; it was a 'hard thing. . .to bring the moonlight into a chamber' (III.i.49) so that Pyramus and Thisbe could meet by moonlight. I like to think that this is a joke of Shakespeare's, because in this very play he has already done the trick. He uses the technique of the advertising man, hammering away with repetition not at the level of full consciousness, but 'subliminally', under the threshold, to a listener who has switched off full attention during the commercials – or a playgoer more intent on the actors and their actions than on particular words. So in Act I of *A Midsummer Night's Dream* Shakespeare repeats 'moon' and 'moonlight' and calls up a picture of a moonlit night, the moon 'decking with liquid pearl the bladed grass' (I.i.211), telling the audience what to expect in Act II. Sure enough the fairy who begins it points up at the 'Moone's sphere', and we believe Oberon when he enters saying 'Ill met by moonlight, proud Titania' (II.i.60) and later recalls moonlight when he saw a mermaid by the 'cold moon', the 'wat'ry moon'.

In *Romeo and Juliet* the same device is employed. In II.i it is obviously late, after the feast; Romeo must have gone 'home to bed', it is 'night', Mercutio calls 'Good-night' as he leaves (II.i.4, 31, 39). As Juliet appears above, Romeo hails her as the sun, killing 'the envious moon' shining in the sky (II.ii.4). Gazing up at her he sees the stars beyond, which suggest comparisons with her eyes, and he repeats 'stars' (15, 19) and imagines her eyes illuminating the heavens so that birds would '*think* it were *not* night' (22) – which of course it is. Juliet is glorious to '*this* night' (27), Romeo is '*thus* bescreened in night' (52) and has 'night's cloak' to hide him. 'The mask of night' hides Juliet's blushes, and she is sure that it is not 'light love, Which the dark night' has revealed (106). Romeo tries to swear by '*yonder* blessed moon' but Juliet (also pointing up at it) urges him not to swear by the twice-repeated 'Moon, th' inconstant moon' (109), and she goes on to say 'night', 'good-night' (three times), 'tonight' (117, 120, 123, 126). Romeo, transported, can only say 'O blessèd, blessèd night' (139) and still the word 'night' occurs seven times more, with the associated words silver, dream, repose, rest, sleep.

With remarkable skill Shakespeare makes these words seem to happen inevitably, each for another purpose, while all the time he is using them to establish the time of night. But by now '''Tis almost morning' (II.ii.176) and Romeo hurries off to Friar Lawrence, whom we meet picking herbs and telling us in conventional Elizabethan verse that the 'grey-eyed morn' is dawning (II.iii.1–5). Another, and a fateful, day has begun.

When Juliet is waiting impatiently for the Nurse to return from Romeo, naturally she mentions the time, complaining that she has been waiting from nine o'clock for 'three long hours' – and this also shows that it is afternoon, the day is getting warmer, when (as Benvolio observes) 'these hot days is the mad blood stirring' (III.i.4). It is still afternoon, and the sun must still be in the sky, when Juliet begs Phoebus' steeds to gallop faster, and 'bring in cloudy night immediately' (III.ii.4).

Whenever time is mentioned, it has an ostensible purpose, as well as keeping the audience hurrying along with the characters. Capulet is talking to Paris 'very late' (III.iv.5). Lady Capulet says she will talk to Juliet 'early tomorrow' (10) but Capulet insists twice that his wife goes 'ere you go to bed' (17, 31) and says 'It is so very late That we may call it early' (34). All these references are suitably prosaic. But for the lovers Shakespeare establishes the time with some exquisite poetry (see page 76). They must part. Juliet will not admit that the dawn has come, until Romeo says that he will stay, if she wishes it, though it means death. The Nurse warns them that Lady Capulet is coming, and that 'the day is broke' (III.v.40). Time rushes on.

Juliet's false repentance makes her father advance the wedding by twenty-four hours, to Wednesday, and all Tuesday night Capulet is fussing about the preparations: 'the second cock hath crowed'. . .''tis three o'clock' . . .'Good faith, 'tis day' (IV.iv.3, 4, 21).

But it is a day not of rejoicing, but of mourning. Romeo hears the news in Mantua, and in less than twenty-four hours more all is ended.

8 HOW THE PLAY IS WRITTEN

'Blank verse' is sometimes thought of as monotonous unrhymed ten-syllabled lines, going ti-tum, ti-tum, ti-tum, ti-tum, ti-tum. But *Romeo and Juliet* illustrates not only the very great variety of rhythms which 'blank verse' can comprehend, but also Shakespeare's skill with prose, and with various sorts of rhymed verse (particularly in the first part of the play): couplets, stanzas and sonnets. And in this most lyrical of his plays he wrote several passages which, though completely relevant in the play, can be enjoyed as poems even if detached from it: Mercutio's 'Queen Mab' speech (I.iv.53–103), Juliet's epithalamium or 'wedding song' (III.ii.1–31) and the aubade or 'dawn song' when the lovers part (III.v.1–36) (see pages 22, 73 and 76).

8.1 VARIETIES OF BLANK VERSE

In the first scene of the play, introduced by the everyday prose of the servingmen, the quick, straightforward verse of the assembling Montagues and Capulets is in strong contrast to the heavy, grandiloquent speech of the authoritative and outraged Prince:

> Rebellious subjects, enemies to peace,
> Profaners of this neighbour-stainèd steel. . .   (I.i.83)

How the atmosphere changes when Benvolio and Montague describe the lovelorn Romeo in fluent conventional love-poetry.

To appreciate the varieties of movement within the blank verse line, read aloud the first hundred lines of Act I, scene v. After the naturalistic prose of the servingmen clearing the dishes comes Capulet, greeting his invited and uninvited guests, cracking jokes about corns, glancing back at his youth (but ''Tis gone, 'tis gone, 'tis gone'), calling commands to the servants. Clearly the speed varies, and punctuation and pauses occur within the lines, not only or necessarily at their ends, thus breaking up the regular rhythm. Romeo's rapturous appraisement of Juliet, 'O she doth teach the torches to burn bright' is still 'blank verse' but totally different in feeling, slow and enchanted, and is followed immediately by Tybalt's fiery intervention and quarrel with Capulet. Capulet's attempts to calm or at least repress Tybalt, to encourage the dancers and to order 'More light!' are yet contained in blank verse form. Tybalt's hot four rhyming lines of fury seem to quiver with his rage:

> Patience perforce with wilful choler meeting
> Makes my flesh tremble in their different greeting.
> I will withdraw, but this intrusion shall,
> Now seeming sweet, convert to bitterest gall.   (I.v.90)

They emphasise by contrast the cool beauty of the sonnet spoken by the lovers.

8.2 WORD-PLAY

Whoever is talking, in verse or prose, there is a great deal of word-play. The Elizabethans thought that writing, particularly writing poetry, needed art and craft as well as inspiration. They appreciated the skilful handling of words, and learned at school the use of 'conceits', figures of speech hardly ever mentioned today, from *antanaclasis* to *zeugma*. *Paronomasia*, or punning, was particularly popular. In *Romeo and Juliet*, Professor Mahood has counted over 175 puns, from the crude *collier, choler, collar* of Sampson and Gregory (I.i.2) or Romeo's *flies, fly* (III.ii.41) and his jingle of *concealed lady . . . cancelled love* (III.iii.97), through the flippant word-battles and wisecracks of Romeo and Mercutio (I.iv and II.iv) to the deeply significant description of Mercutio as a *grave man* (III.i.101) and of the clouds *severing* as they divide at sunrise and so giving the signal for the *severing* of the lovers (III.v.8). It is noticeable that the early punning for punning's sake fades away after Mercutio's death, when the whole play darkens. The word-play in the last acts has real meaning: death is *engrossing* as a lawyer making a bargain legal, but also as monopolising and absorbing (V.iii.115).

The simple device of *polyptoton* – repetition of the same word, preferably in a different form – occurs over a hundred times, for instance:

> To wield *old partisans*, in hands as *old*,
>   *Cankered* with peace, to *part* your *cankered* hate.   (I.i.96)

or 'Upon whose brow *shame* is *ashamed* to sit' (III.ii.92)
or 'What less than *doomsday* is the prince's *doom*?' (III.iii.9).

By no means everyone enjoys these conceits. The American critic Mark van Doren remarked of *Romeo and Juliet* that 'its author, no less than its hero and heroine, is furiously literary', and Dr Johnson thought that the conceits 'polluted' Shakespeare's 'pathetic strains'. But the Elizabethans felt very differently: the play is advertised on the title-page of the First Quarto as 'AN EXCELLENT conceited Tragedie', skilfully composed, or as an Elizabethan would have said approvingly, 'artificial' – that is, made with art.

8.3 IMAGES

Poets often convey their meaning by images, by comparing one thing with another, through similes or metaphors. It is a feature of Shakespeare's plays that he sometimes uses clusters of images on the same theme throughout the play, giving the audience its atmosphere and flavour. In *Hamlet* 'something is rotten in the state of Denmark', and there are continual images of disease and corruption.

In *Romeo and Juliet* the dominant imagery is concerned with light – sun, moon, stars, candles, gunpowder, lightning, fire, torches – many times repeated. Paradoxically it is the darkness, the night, which protects the lovers. They meet at night, declare their love at night, spend one night together before cruel day parts them, and die together at night. Love is the light in the darkness of feuding Verona.

While Romeo has an artificial love for Rosaline, he shuts himself in 'an artificial night', his humour is 'black and portentous' (I.i.142), and Benvolio thinks that this love is 'blind, and best befits the dark' (II.i.32). But Juliet 'teaches the torches to burn bright' (I.v.45); she is the sun lightening the darkness (II.ii.2). Romeo and Juliet see each other as sparks of light against the dark; she is a jewel twinkling against black skin; Juliet's eyes are like stars in the night sky, 'so bright That birds would sing and think it were not night' (II.ii.21). When she leaves the balcony, 'light' is gone (II.ii.155). Romeo in his turn is seen as stars 'making the face of heaven so fine' and as 'day in night' (III.ii.23, 17).

Their love is a different kind of llight, a dangerous light, 'too like the lightning' (II.ii.119) or 'fire and powder Which as they kiss consume' (II.vi.10). When Romeo and Tybalt fight: 'To it they go like lightning' (III.i.176) and finally Romeo seeks a poison that will act as swiftly and as 'violently as hasty powder fired' (V.i.64).

And at the end of the play, when the parents' hopes and joys are extinguished, even nature mourns in darkness: 'The sun for sorrow will not show his head' (V.iii.305).

Of course there are also many other images of every imaginable kind, drawn from animals, the sea, food, war, illness, sport, religion, law

Dr Caroline Spurgeon has counted and analysed more than 200. In the later plays Shakespeare rarely uses an image which is not integrated into the whole meaning of the speech or scene where it occurs. But in *Romeo and Juliet* he piles one image on another, giving the same richly decorated effect found in jewels, clothes and embroideries of the same period. Just as Juliet pictures night in many forms (see page 74), so Romeo, in the speech before his suicide, pictures death (V.iii.92): first as a bee-like lover who has 'sucked the honey' of Juliet's breath, though death, as a warrior, has not yet conquered her and has not replaced beauty's crimson flag by his own pale standard. Death is a monster, Juliet's gaoler; death is a lawyer, sealing a final, all-embracing bargain. The final lines can be interpreted in different ways. The 'bitter conduct' [conductor], 'unsavoury guide' may be death yet again, or perhaps the poison. The whole passage is reminiscent of the *Dance of Death* by Holbein, Henry VIII's court painter, a series of woodcuts in which death comes in many guises to every sort of man from emperor to beggar.

There are many other images in the speech, including a notable double meaning. When Romeo promises to 'set up my everlasting rest' it clearly means that he will stay there for ever. But in the Elizabethan gambling game primero, to 'set up one's rest' was to stake everything one had. By committing suicide Romeo is venturing all he has: his life, and his immortal soul. Ironically Shakespeare uses the same image to comic effect, when the Nurse coarsely and jocularly says to the drugged Juliet

> . . .for the next night I warrant
> The County Paris hath set up his rest
> That you shall rest but little.   (IV.v.5)

8.4 LYRIC POETRY

The three plays which Shakespeare wrote about the same time, *Richard II*, *A Midsummer Night's Dream* and *Romeo and Juliet*, are full of lyric poetry which carries on the drama, but can also be detached and enjoyed for its own sake.

Shakespeare had already written the two long narrative poems, *Venus and Adonis* and *The Rape of Lucrece*, in six-line stanzas rhyming a b a b c c. Romeo (I.ii.89) and Benvolio (I.ii.46, 95), exchanging comments on love, and Paris in his formal lament over Juliet (V.iii.12) recite stanzas of mediocre quality. More meaningfully, the Prince's last words (V.iii.304) are in the form of a similar stanza, when the neat shape of the verse rounds off the play:

> A glooming peace this morning with it brings;
>> The sun for sorrow will not show his head.
> Go hence to have more talk of these sad things;
>> Some shall be pardoned and some punishèd.
> For never was a story of more woe
> Than this of Juliet and her Romeo.

This was curiously misquoted at the end of the Franco Zefferelli film of *Romeo and Juliet*, because punishèd was pronounced with only two syllables – giving a very odd, unfinished effect, and emphasising the importance of Shakespeare's rhythmic patterns.

Mercutio's 'Queen Mab' speech (I.iv.53–103) falls into two parts, a brilliant satire on society, and a short meditation on dreams – neither essential to the play, more like arias in an opera which give a prima donna a chance to exhibit her powers. Another 'set piece' is Juliet's 'vial' speech (IV.iii.15–58). It is too melodramatic for some tastes, but again gives the player a splendid chance to exhibit virtuosity (see page 42).

The most important form of love poetry in the 1590s was the sonnet; many poets, including Edmund Spenser, Sir Philip Sidney and Shakespeare, wrote long sequences, sometimes of a hundred or more. A Shakespearean sonnet was a poem of fourteen lines, arranged in three groups each of four lines, with a clinching couplet at the end. The rhyming went a b a b; c d c d; e f e f; g g. Shakespeare used this form, so complete in itself, for the two Choruses; for the first meeting of Romeo with Juliet he chose a sonnet full of religious imagery, to emphasise the innocence of both the lovers (see page 23).

8.5 CRITICAL ANALYSIS OF TWO PASSAGES

Two important passages must be looked at in greater detail: first Juliet's soliloquy, III.ii.1–31.

In the most famous of Elizabethan epithalamiums, or wedding songs, Edmund Spenser wrote:

> Ah when will this long weary day have end,
> And give me leave to come unto my love?. . .
> Haste thee O fairest Planet to thy home
> Within the Western foam;
> Thy tired steeds long since have need of rest.

Juliet, eagerly waiting for night and Romeo, uses the same image: the sun as chariot of the god Phoebus Apollo. But it is used with much more urgency and elaboration:

> Gallop apace, you fiery-footed steeds
> Towards Phoebus' lodging; such a waggoner
> As Phaeton would whip you to the west,
> And bring in cloudy night immediately.   (III.ii.1)

Phaeton was Apollo's son, who tried to drive the chariot of the sun, and nearly let it fall down to the earth at high noon, bringing night. Juliet invokes the longed-for night in a rapid succession of images:

> Spread thy close curtain, love-performing night,
> That runaways eyes may wink, and Romeo
> Leap to these arms, untalked of and unseen.

First a servant, drawing cloud-curtains of darkness over the sky, like bed-curtains round an Elizabethan four-poster, so that Romeo may secretly 'leap' to her arms. 'Leap' continues the sense of urgency. 'Night' is 'love-performing', the time for love-making.

> Lovers can see to do their amorous rites
> By their own beauties; or if love be blind,
> It best agrees with night. Come civil night,
> Thou sober-suited matron all in black,
> And learn me how to lose a winning match,
> Played for a pair of stainless maidenhoods.

No artificial light is required: 'dark night is Cupid's day', wrote Christopher Marlowe. The lovers themselves are radiant and light-giving: this is echoed sadly when Romeo declares that the dead Juliet still makes her tomb 'a feasting presence full of light' (V.iii.84). Next, night becomes a well-behaved and wise woman, who will teach Juliet how to play and win the game – or battle, 'Hymen's war', Ben Jonson calls it – of love; both lovers will lose their virginity, through winning love. But Juliet blushes easily – when the Nurse brought news of Romeo the 'wanton blood' made her cheeks 'scarlet' (II.v.71) – and now she feels herself blushing at her frank thoughts:

> Hood my unmanned blood, bating in my cheeks,
> With thy black mantle, till strange love grown bold,
> Think true love acted simple modesty.

Her blood is 'bating', fluttering like the wings of a hawk; night must be the falconer who tames the 'unmanned', unbroken, hawk by making it wear a hood; night's cloak must hide and hood the blushes of the 'unmanned' virgin, Juliet, until the power of true love paradoxically makes 'strange' love, unfamiliar and shy, grow bold, and its physical expression seem simple and modest.

> Come night, come Romeo, come thou day in night;
> For thou wilt lie upon the wings of night,
> Whiter than snow upon a raven's back.

As Juliet in the orchard was to Romeo the rising sun, so Romeo's coming will turn night to day. Juliet thinks of an extreme contrast – white snow on black feathers – just as he has seen her as a 'snowy dove trooping with crows' (I.v.49). In the orchard, Romeo thought of Juliet's eyes as brighter than stars – stars which are but sparks of light, but are permanent – now she utters a conceit even more extravagant, but which carries conviction because of her intensity:

> Give me my Romeo, and when he shall die,
> Take him and cut him out in little stars,
> And he will make the face of heaven so fine
> That all the world will be in love with night
> And pay no worship to the garish sun.

Then Juliet's impatience breaks through, and she expresses it in merchandising terms, as Romeo did when he said that he would travel to the ends of the earth for her (II.ii.82).

> O I have bought the mansion of a love,
> But not possessed it, and though I am sold,
> Not yet enjoyed. So tedious is this day
> As is the night before some festival
> To an impatient child that hath new robes
> And may not wear them.

In her eagerness she is at once merchant and merchandise. And then we are reminded how very young she is, in the image of the child longing for the never-ending eve of a festival to pass. The thrice-repeated 'not. . .not. . .not' (27, 28, 31) suggests that her anticipated joy will not materialise. Other repetitions strengthen the passage: '*Come night, come* Romeo, *come* thou day in *night*' (17) with its strong monosyllables, is echoed less vehemently: '*Come* gentle *night, come* loving black-browed *night*' (30) and indeed the key-word 'night' occurs eleven times in this speech, while 'love', 'lovers' and 'loving' occur eight times, showing Juliet's thoughts and feelings very clearly. Echoes such as 'unseen', 'see' (7), or 'unmanned', 'mantle' (14) often occur. Note too how *alliteration*, repeated use of words that begin with the same letter, is used: 'By', 'beauties', 'blind', 'best' (9–10); 'sober-suited' (11); 'learn', 'lose' (12); 'played', 'pair' (13); 'blood', 'bating', 'black', 'bold' (14). *Assonance*, the use of similar accented vowels, with different consonants, for instance 'pair', 'stainless', 'maidenhoods' (13), and *rhyme* are also used to delight the ear. None of these devices are obtrusive; we feel the total effect of the whole passage, and only later can examine it and try to discover what means Shakespeare used to achieve his ends.

Juliet's ecstasy of love is interrupted by the Nurse's entrance, bringing the ruin of their hopes. The next passage of lyrical verse to be noticed will be spoken as the lovers part for ever (III.v.1–11).

This aubade begins with an elaborate pattern of repeated words and phrases, again unobtrusive, but most effective:

> JULIET: Wilt thou be gone? It is not yet near day,
> It was the nightingale, and not the lark
> That pierced the fearful hollow of thine ear.
> Nightly she sings on yon pomegranate tree.
> Believe me, love, it was the nightingale.
> ROMEO: It was the lark, the herald of the morn,
> No nightingale. Look, love, what envious streaks
> Do lace the severing clouds in yonder east.
> Night's candles are burnt out, and jocund day
> Stands tiptoe on the misty mountain tops.

It is dawn. But Juliet will not believe that it is time to part. She searches frantically for an excuse to keep Romeo with her, but it is clear that she is deliberately deceiving herself. They have been so close that Romeo's ear appeared as a 'hollow' to her – 'fearful', full of fear, because they must have been listening all night in case they were discovered. Now it has been 'pierced', painfully, as if stabbed by a thin sharp instrument, by the shrill song of the lark – the traditional soft 'jug-jug' of the nightingale could not 'pierce' anything. 'Pomegranate tree' reminds us that we are in Italy, and instead of a cold northern dawn 'in russet mantle clad' (*Hamlet*, I.i.166), 'jocund day' (in reality bringing misery) 'stands tiptoe on the misty mountain tops'.

The clouds are 'severing', that is, parting, as must the lovers – and are edged with gold. The stars, 'night's candles', are *'burnt* out' – not 'blown out', to be relighted, but finally extinguished. Romeo sums up in an elegant antithesis, which is also totally simple and sincere:

> ROMEO: I must be gone and live, or stay and die.
> JULIET: Yon light is not daylight; I know it, I.
> It is some meteor that the sun exhaled
> To be to thee this night a torch-bearer,
> And light thee on thy way to Mantua.
> Therefore stay yet, thou need'st not to be gone.

ROMEO: Let me be ta'en, let me be put to death;
        I am content, so thou wilt have it so.
        I'll say yon gray is not the morning's eye,
        'Tis but the pale reflex of Cynthia's brow.

Juliet persists; the light is but a passing meteor, not the coming dawn.
Romeo suddenly makes a courtly surrender to his lady's will; he agrees
that the lightening sky is not caused by 'the morning's eye', the sun, but is
merely a reflection of the moon.

ROMEO: Nor that is not the lark whose notes do beat
        The vaulty heaven so high above our heads.
        I have more care to stay than will to go.
        Come death and welcome! Juliet wills it so.
        How is't?, my soul? Let's talk; it is not day.
JULIET: It is, it is, hie hence, be gone, away.
        It is the lark that sings so out of tune,
        Straining harsh discords, and unpleasing sharps.
        Some say the lark makes sweet division;
        This doth not so, for she divideth us.

To please Juliet, Romeo pretends that it is not the lark, while unmistakably
describing the strong vibrations of the continuous lark song, still 'beating'
and being reflected from the 'vaulty heaven', the great arch of the sky.
Juliet admits, hopelessly, that it is indeed the lark, and therefore unwel-
come – 'out of tune', shrill, 'harsh' and 'unpleasing'. A 'division was a
descant of short quick notes. How can the lark's 'division' be sweet, when
it divides her from Romeo?

   We can see from all these examples that in *Romeo and Juliet* Shakespeare
is experimenting with a great variety of styles, from the coarsest realistic
prose to the most formal poetry. Everywhere we find conceits, wordplay,
images. If we look at the elaborately embroidered clothes, or the elaborately
carved screens and tombs of the 1590s, we can see that this play is another
example of the Elizabethan passion for splendour, for filling every corner
with decoration. And yet perhaps the most moving moments, as in
Shakespeare's later plays, are those of complete simplicity.

9 CRITICAL RECEPTION

Romeo and Juliet has always been very popular on the stage (see page 61). Literary critics have approved less whole-heartedly, occupying themselves with academic questions, such as whether *Romeo and Juliet* is a true 'tragedy'. Theatre audiences, experiencing the living play, have no doubts. This section introduces the ideas of some twentieth-century critics, whose works are listed on page 85.

H. Granville-Barker, scholar as well as actor and producer, in a valuable study of every aspect of the play, concludes that it is a 'tragedy of mischance' and that the final disasters are due to 'opportunity muddled away and marred by ill-luck', though he does not ignore the contributing factor of Romeo's rash impulsiveness.

H. Granville-Barker, scholar as well as actor and producer, in a valuable 'tragedies'. The usual protagonist was a powerful man, often a king or general, whose downfall (caused by some inherent flaw in his nature) brought ruin on the surrounding society as well as on himself. But in Shakespeare's *Romeo and Juliet* we are shown two young lovers, almost children, whose deaths eventually heal the wounds of a strife-torn society. In addition the play begins with two light-hearted acts of comedy, and not till Mercutio's death in Act III does tragedy intrude. Charlton thinks too much depends on 'fate' and 'fortune', and argues that Romeo and Juliet are the unfortunate victims of accident, rather than flawed tragic protagonists.

G. I. Duthie blames malicious fate, and sees the families, rather than the lovers, as the principal protagonists. Their warring is to blame. J. Nosworthy goes further still in refusing to recognise the play as a tragedy, because it contains too much comedy, and because he thinks the feud is insufficiently emphasised. But we may think it almost absurd to *read* the play, and then denigrate it on theoretical grounds, while in the theatre audiences, voting with their feet, throng to see it acted.

APPENDIX: SHAKESPEARE'S THEATRE

We should speak, as Muriel Bradbrook reminds us, not of the Elizabethan stage but of Elizabethan stages. Plays of Shakespeare were acted on tour, in the halls of mansions, one at least in Gray's Inn, frequently at Court, and after 1609 at the Blackfriars, a small roofed theatre for those who could afford the price. But even after his Company acquired the Blackfriars, we know of no play of his not acted (unless, rather improbably, *Troilus* is an exception) for the general public at the Globe, or before 1599 at its predecessor, The Theatre, which, since the Globe was constructed from the same timbers must have resembled it. Describing the Globe, we can claim therefore to be describing, in an acceptable sense, Shakespeare's theatre, the physical structure his plays were designed to fit. Even in the few probably written for a first performance elsewhere, adaptability to that structure would be in his mind.

For the facilities of the Globe we have evidence from the drawing of the Swan theatre (based on a sketch made by a visitor to London about 1596) which depicts the interior of another public theatre; the builder's contract for the Fortune theatre, which in certain respects (fortunately including the dimensions and position of the stage) was to copy the Globe; indications in the dramatic texts; comments, like Ben Jonson's on the throne let down from above by machinery; and eye-witness testimony to the number of spectators (in round figures, 3,000) accommodated in the auditorium.

In communicating with the audience, the actor was most favourably placed. Soliloquising at the centre of the front of the great platform, he was at the mid-point of the theatre, with no-one among the spectators more than sixty feet away from him. That platform-stage (Figs I and II) was the most important feature for performance at the Globe. It had the audience – standing in the yard (10) and seated in the galleries (9) – on three sides of it. It was 43 feet wide, and 27½ feet from front to back. Raised (?5½ feet) above the level of the yard, it had a trap-door (II.8) giving access to the space below it. The actors, with their equipment, occupied the 'tiring house' (attiring-house: 2) immediately at the back of the stage. The stage-direction 'within' means inside the tiring-house. Along its frontage, probably from the top of the second storey, juts out the canopy or 'Heavens', carried on two large pillars rising through the platform (6, 7) and sheltering the rear part of the stage, the rest of which, like the yard, was open to the sky. If the 'hut' (I.8), housing the machinery for descents, stood, as in the Swan drawing, above the 'Heavens', that covering must have had a trap-door, so that the descents could be made through it.

Descents are one illustration of the vertical dimension the dramatist could use to supplement the playing-area of the great platform. The other opportunities are provided by the tiring-house frontage or façade. About this façade the evidence is not as complete or clear as we should like, so that Fig. I is in part conjectural. Two doors giving entry to the platform there certainly were (3). A third (4) is probable but not certain. When curtained, a door, most probably this one, would furnish what must be termed a discovery-space (II.5), not an inner stage (on which action in any depth would have been out of sight for a significant part of the audience). Usually no more than two actors were revealed (exceptionally, three), who often then moved out on to the platform. An example of this is Ferdinand and Miranda in *The Tempest* 'discovered' at chess, then seen on the platform speaking with their fathers. Similarly the gallery (I.5) was not an upper stage. Its use was not limited to the actors; sometimes it functioned as 'lords' rooms' for favoured spectators, sometimes, perhaps, as a musicians' gallery. Frequently the whole gallery would not be needed for what took place aloft: a window-stage (as in the first balcony scene in *Romeo*, even perhaps in the second) would suffice. Most probably this would be a part (at one end) of the gallery itself; or just possibly, if the gallery did not (as it does in the Swan drawing) extend the whole width of the tiring-house, a window over the left- or right-hand door. As the texts show, whatever was presented aloft, or in the discovery-space, was directly related to the action on the platform, so that at no time was there left, between the audience and the action of the drama, a great bare space of platform-stage. In relating Shakespeare's drama to the physical conditions of the theatre, the primacy of that platform is never to be forgotten.

Note: The present brief account owes most to C. Walter Hodges, *The Globe Restored*; Richard Hosley in *A New Companion to Shakespeare Studies*, and in *The Revels History of English Drama*; and to articles by Hosley and Richard Southern in *Shakespeare Survey*, 12, 1959, where full discussion can be found.

HAROLD BROOKS

SHAKESPEARE'S THEATRE

The stage and its adjuncts; the tiring-house; and the auditorium.

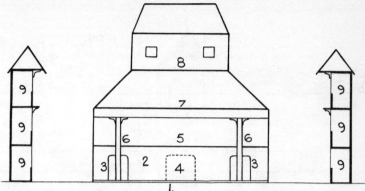

FIG I ELEVATION

1. Platform stage (approximately five feet above the ground) 2. Tiring-house
3. Tiring-house doors to stage 4. Conjectural third door 5. Tiring-house
gallery (balustrade and partitioning not shown) 6. Pillars supporting the
heavens 7. The heavens 8. The hut 9. The spectators' galleries

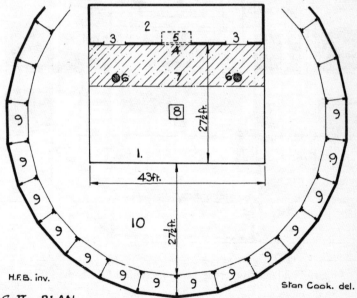

H.F.B. inv.

Stan Cook. del.

FIG II PLAN

1. Platform stage 2. Tiring-house 3. Tiring-house doors to stage
4. Conjectural third door 5. Conjectural discovery space (alternatively behind 3)
6. Pillars supporting the heavens 7. The heavens 8. Trap door 9. Spectators'
gallery 10. The yard

The Globe

An artist's imaginative recreation of a typical Elizabethan theatre

FURTHER READING

William Shakespeare
S. Schoenbaum, *William Shakespeare: A Documentary Life* (Oxford University Press, 1975). The definitive life of Shakespeare, reproducing every document known to have any connection with him.

Elizabethan Theatre
G. E. Bentley, *The Profession of Dramatist in Shakespeare's Time* (Princeton, 1971) pp. 113–44, 264–8. By the greatest living authority on this subject.
H. R. Hoppe, *The Bad Quarto of 'Romeo and Juliet'* (New York: Ithaca, 1948). An elaborate and detailed study.
S. Schoenbaum, see above.

Sources and Themes
G. Bullough, *Narrative and Dramatic Sources of Shakespeare* (London, 1957) vol. 1, pp. 269–363. Full account of the many sources of the plot; long extracts from Brooke's *Romeus and Juliet*.
H. B. Charlton, *Shakespearean Tragedy* (Cambridge, 1948) pp. 49–63. *Romeo and Juliet* as a new kind of tragedy.
N. Coghill, *Shakespeare's Professional Skills* (Cambridge, 1964) pp. 28–31. Two examples of Shakespeare's transformation of Brooke.
K. Muir, *The Sources of Shakespeare's Plays* (Methuen, 1977) pp. 38–46. Admirable brief account of sources including passages from Sidney and Daniel.

Characterisation
S. T. Coleridge, *Lectures on Shakespeare and Milton (1812)*. Lecture VII.
F. Dickey, *Not Wisely but too Well* (California: San Marino, 1966). Very much against Romeo.

H. Granville-Barker, *Prefaces to Shakespeare* (London 1930) vol. II, pp. 41–66. Gives the actor's viewpoint.

D. A. Stauffer, *Shakespeare's World of Images* (New York, 1949). The lovers as innocent victims.

The Play on the Stage

J. R. Brown, 'S. Franco Zefferelli's *Romeo and Juliet*' in *Shakespeare Survey 15* (1962). An examination of the famous film.

H. Granville-Barker, see above, pp. 31–46. On staging and costume.

A. Gurr, *The Shakespearean Stage 1574–1642* (Cambridge, 1970). A lucid summary of the ascertainable facts.

C. W. Hodges, *The Globe Restored* (London, 1968) 2nd edn. Clear and straightforward, with good illustrations.

G. C. D. Odell, *Shakespeare from Betterton to Irving* (London, 1920, reprinted New York, 1963). Descriptions of early productions.

A. C. Sprague, *Shakespeare and the Actors* (Cambridge Mass., 1944; New York, 1963) pp. 297–319.

J. L. Styan, *Shakespeare's Stagecraft* (Cambridge, 1967). Re-creations of parts of *Romeo and Juliet* on the Elizabethan stage.

C. B. Young, 'Stage History' in the New Cambridge edition of *Romeo and Juliet* (1961) pp. xxxviii–liii.

How the Play is Written

W. H. Clemen, *The Development of Shakespeare's Imagery* (Methuen, 1951; University Paperback, 1966) pp. 63–73. The change from a conventional to a more spontaneous style as seen in *Romeo and Juliet*.

M. A. Mahood, *Shakespeare's Wordplay* (Methuen, 1957; University Paperback, 1968) pp. 56–72. Ingenious and thorough study.

C. E. Spurgeon, *Shakespeare's Imagery* (Cambridge, 1935). The pioneer work on the subject. Use the index to find relevant passages on *Romeo and Juliet*.

Critical Reception

M. C. Bradbrook, *Shakespeare and Elizabethan Poetry* (London, 1951).

E. D. Cole (ed.), *Twentieth Century Interpretations of 'Romeo and Juliet'* (Englewood Cliffs N.J., 1970). Contains a selection of writings on the play, including parts of Granville Barker, Levin, Spurgeon.

G. I. Duthie, 'Introduction' to *Romeo and Juliet* (Cambridge, 1935).

H. Levin, 'Form and Formality in *Romeo and Juliet*' in *Shakespeare Quarterly XI* (1960).

J. Nosworthy, 'The Two Angry Families of Verona' in *Shakespeare Quarterly III* (1952).

V. K. Whitaker, *The Mirror up to Nature* (California: San Marino, 1965).